WORD IS BOND

DON KILAM TRUST CO.

Secrets Of Bond & Being Released With A Signature

Lets start this out by saying in order to win in court you have to know what goes on in court. What goes on in the court rooms goes back to **Edward the First** - it's called **Statute Merchant** and what it is, is a **Bond of Merchant** or **Bond of Record**. The statutes themselves are the **Bond** and what they do is duplicate the **statutes** that they charge you under with what they call a **Recognizance Bond** and people sign the **Recognizance Bond** without reading what the **Bond** says. When you go into court on a criminal charge, it's **CIVIL NOT CRIMINAL**.

What they're doing **is all about Bonds**. When you go into the courtroom after you're arrested they use two different sets of Bonds. What they do when your arrested they fill out a "***Bid Bond***". The **United States District Court** uses **273, 274 & 275**. SF means "**Standard Form**". Standard Form 273, Standard Form 274 & Standard Form 275. This is the United States District court. There is another set of Bonds and they are all put out by GSA.; General Services Administration. GSA Form SF24 is the "**Bid Bond**", everyone should have a copy of the Bid Bond. The "**Performance Bond**" is SF25. The "**Payment Bond**" is SF25A and put out by the General Services Administration which is abbreviated GSA. The GSA is under the "Comptroller of the Currency" which is under the GAO, the "General Accounting Office". O.K. you have two sets of Bonds: SF24, SF25 & SF25A. At the Federal Level you have SF273, SF274 & SF275.

What are they doing with these Bonds? What's going on in the courtroom is that they are suing you for a debt collection. What it is, is an action of "**ASSUMPSIT**" The word "**PRESUME**" comes from the word "Assumpsit" which means "I agree or I presume to do". An act of "Assumpsit" which means "**I agree to a collection of a debt**". If you look at these Bonds...everyone of these Bonds:The "**Bid Bond**", "**Performance Bond**" & "**Payment Bond**" all have a "**PENAL SUM**" attached to it. The reason for the "Penal Sum" is if you don't pay the Debt, you go into "**Default Judgment**". That is what is going on in the courtroom. **That is why all of these guys are sitting in prison wondering what's going on**. If you go in there and argue jurisdiction...Jack Smith is exactly correct in what he is saying about the **HONOR & DISHONOR**. If you go in and argue jurisdiction or refuse to answer questions that the judge or the court addresses to you, they will find you in **contempt** of court and they will put you in jail and if you read "Clerks Praxis" that's all they talk about is contempt. What they used to do back in **Edward the 1st**; if you owed a Debt they would send a Sheriff out with a **Warrant** to arrest you. This is **ALL CIVIL**, this is **NOT CRIMINAL**. It's just a **smoke screen** to cover up what they are doing with **Mercantile Civil Law** and what they used to do when they arrested people with a warrant and brought the person into court and made them sign a **Bond** to release until the civil suit commenced. It actually says "**Civil Suit**" in "Clerks Praxis". This is how you spell "**Clerk's Praxis**". Latin for "**Practice**", if you look up "Praxis" it means "Practice"

With The Admin process one must start with a **Letters of Rogatory**"; this is a foreign letter to the court which breaks down the behind the scene facts about the collection of the debt. What they do is arrest you, then they hold you...basically they hold you until the suit has been completed and when they get "**Default Judgment**" on you because of failure to pay the Debt, they put you in prison. Attorneys are there to cover up the smoke screen. What attorneys do, because no-one knows what's going on, **they lead you into"Dishonor"** or "**Default Judgment**" and then the court puts you into prison **then they sell your "Default Judgment"**. Who do they sell it to?

Believe it or not, the <u>U.S. District Court buys all of these State Court Judgments</u>. Get on a search engine and type in U.S. Courts. After you get to the US Courts, go to the 11th Circuit Court of the United States…Circuit 1 thru Circuit 11. Click on **<u>Circuit 7</u>**. That will take you into the various courts; Bankruptcy, District etc. Click on to the **Northern Illinois District Court**; that will take you to the Clerk's office - there's a box there, then scroll down and you'll see "**Administrative Offices**" where you'll see "**Financial Department**". It will talk about the "**<u>Criminal Justice Act</u>**" and "**<u>Optional Bids</u>**" and this is all spelled out and their not trying to hide it. Go down to "**<u>List of Sureties</u>**" it will have "**<u>FMS.Treas.gov</u>**", this is the **<u>Department of Treasury</u>**. When you get into the Department of Treasury you see on the left hand side of the screen you'll see "**<u>Admitted Reinsure</u>**" and underneath that will be a "**<u>List of Sureties</u>**" then under that, the word "**<u>Forms</u>**".

From there you'll see about **300** "**reinsurance**" companies, they're all 'insurance" companies. There are two sets of companies: a list of "Surety" and "Reinsurance" companies. Under 750 of the Department of Treasury, they have to be **certified** so they can buy up these Bonds; these are the people that are buying these Bonds when you went into "**Default Judgment**" and they can't buy these Bonds unless they are Certified by the Secretary of the Treasury.

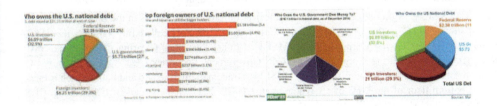

Next, click onto the word "**Forms**" and it will take you to the "**Miller Act**" reinsurance and will list 3 different kinds of Bonds. They don't use a "Bid Bond" in the District Court that's why we are utilizing a "Form 24". All of these Forms come out of the GSA, the General Services Administration. Form 24, 25, 25A and 273, 274 & 275. The 273, 274 & 275 Bond forms; the 273 is the Reinsurance with the United States. The 274 is the Miller Act reinsurance "**Performance Bond**". The 275 is your "Payment Bond", your Miller Act Reinsurance **Payment Bond**. What are they doing with these Bonds?

If you go into these regulations, what they are telling you is, they are buying up **commercial items**; they use the word commercial items and in 2.01 of these regulations… these regulations are divided up into 50 parts. There's 1126 pages in volume I and 823 pages in volume II and their all on the disc and what they tell in there is 2.01 defines commercial items as **non personal property**. What is non personal property? Any property that is not real-estate - it means <u>immovable</u>, real-estate is not movable. Go into your Uniform Commercial Code and look up the word movable and immovables.

This thing is really good…basically what it says is…"**Commercial Paper; Negotiable Instruments…** anything you put your signature on is a Negotiable Instrument under the Uniform Commercial Code which is the Lex Mercantorium. Its Merchantile Civil Law and the reason they use Lex Merchantorium in the court room is because everyone of you are Merchant's at Law and Merchants at Law is anyone whom hold themselves out to be an expert because you use commercial paper; because you use commercial paper on a day to day schedule; you are considered to be an expert and this is why they are not telling you what is going on in the courtroom because you are presumed to know this because you hold yourself out to be an expert because you use commercial paper all the time. Everytime you put your signature on a piece of paper, you are creating a Negotiable Instrument. Some are Non-Negotiable and some are Negotiable. Everytime you endorse something your acting as an accommodation party or an accommodation maker under 3-419. An accommodation party is anyone who loans their signature to another party. Read UCC 3-419, it tells you what an accommodation maker is and what an accommodation party is. When you loan your signature to them they can re-write your signature on any document they want and that's what they are doing. This is what is going on and what the Federal Courts are doing they are buying up these state court default judgments and these are called criminal cases, but are actually civil cases and call them criminal to cover up what they are doing. If you read "Clerk's Praxis" you find that what they call criminal is all civil, they just call it criminal to cover up what their doing. If you don't pay the debt you go to prison bottom line,

C.U.S.I.P. # = Committee on Uniform Identification Process. CUSIP is in the DTC building on 55 Water street. **DTC** <u>is the Depository</u> Trust Corporation. It's also called the: **GFCC**; the **DTCC**: <u>Depository</u> Trust Clear<u>ing Corporation</u> the **MSCC**: <u>Mutual</u> <u>Securities Clearing Corporation</u>. **NSCC**: <u>National Security</u> Clear<u>ing Corporation</u>. **GSCC**: <u>Government</u> <u>Securities Clearing Corporation;</u> One Trillion dollars a day goes through the DTC. CUSIP is a trademark of Standard and Poors which is located on the bottom floor of the DTC of 55 Waterstreet. CUSIP has what is called C.I.N.S. = CUSIP INTERNATIONAL NUMBERING SYSTEM.

For domestic they have a 6 digit numbering system and when they go international which is where CINS comes in and ISID = International Securities Identification Division. It's called ISIDPLUS and theyhave a Global Networking System that includes Paine Webber which has 10,000 corporations in it; they are the major stockholder in CCA which is Correction Corporations of America and they are in Nashville Tennessee. Everyone should have this list and what they have done is privatized the system; everything, even real-estate; Ginny Mae, Fanny Mae all of HUD…all of your…this is international. **<u>EVERYBODY IS FEEDING OFF OF THE PRISON SYSTEM; ALL OF THE MAJOR CORPORATIONS ARE FEEDING OFF OF THE PRISON SYSTEM.</u>**

REIT = Real Estate Investment Trust or PZN which means Prison Trust. They own all the real estate because they hold the Bonds on them. You haven't redeemed your Bond so they didn't close your account. Here's what goes on: A contractor comes in or any corporation could come in and what they do is tender a Bid Bond to the US District Court and they buy up these court judgments and anytime you issue a Bid Bond there has to be a reinsure; they even have a Reinsurance Treaty…International Treaties. If you read the Constitution, Treaties are the Supreme Law of the land. So they get a Reinsurance Company to come in and act as Surety for the Bid Bond then they bring in a Performance Bond. All of these Bonds; Bid, Payment & Performance are Surety Bonds and anytime you issue a Bid Bond it has to have a Surety. Where is the Surety going? It's guaranteeing or reinsuring the Bid Bond by issuing a Performance Bond…that's what these Performance Bonds are. Then they get an underwriter and that would be either an Investment Broker or an Investment Banker; they come in and underwrite the Performance Bond which is reinsuring the Bid Bond.

What does the underwriter do with the Payment Bond? The underwriter takes the 3 Bonds and pools them and known as **Mortgaged Backed Securities** and when you pool these MBS they're called BONDS and they're sold to a company called TBA which is the Bond Market Association - this is an actual Corporation. What they do is after the Payment Bond is issued to reinsure or underwrite the Performance Bond which reinsures the Bid Bond, they convert these Bonds to investment securities…the banks do and Brokerage houses and they sell these as investment securities and you are **funding the whole process because you got into Default Judgment when you went into court.**

Before you can do anything you have to know what's going on and there are regulations which are at 48 CFR Code of Federal Regulations. This is where all of this information is coming from. .Part 12 deals with commercial items and commercial items are Negotiable Instruments and their selling these court judgments as Negotiable Instruments as commercial Items through these Bonds: The Bid Bond, the Performance Bond and the Payment Bond. What is a "Reinsure"? Anytime your dealing in Bonds or "Risk Management" and what the "Reinsure" is doing is insuring part of the risk of the Bid Bond. What they do is give him a portion of the original premium; this is all insurance. The original insurer gives him a part of the premium of the policy of the Bid Bond in exchange for being a "Reinsure" or indemnity or act as surety for the Bid Bond. Then the underwriter comes in and guarantees the resale of the Bonds back to the Public as investment securities.

In order to win in court you have to redeem the Bond. Go in and ask them for the Bond everyone will disappear; nobody will show up…Ask them for the Bid Bond Back, ask for full settlement and closure of the account. Securities & Exchange Commission or the S.E.C. is the next stop for the bonds that have been converted into Securities as we shall explain further. They take your Bond because you got into Default Judgment because you didn't pay the debt and took your Bond and made an investment security out of it. **Their making a fortune off you**.. They go international and when they go International they go as CINS and from CINS they go to ANNA = Annual Numerical Number Association and located in Brussels Belgium and they have unlimited capital. How many of you have heard of **Eurostream**? This is where your Pound, Yen, and Sterling; everything came under the Prison System; everything is being funneled through it. Their all feeding off of it.

Everything is under Lex Mercantoria. If you go into the State Statutes and I don't care what code you go into it will say the principle of **law and equity or law Merchant is the decision in all the courts**; everything is commercial. **72 CFR 27.11 says that all crimes are commercial**. If you read that it says kidnapping, robbery, extortion, murder etc are commercial crimes and if you don't do full settlement and closure of the account, they will put you in prison. What they do is they <u>sell the Bond both domestically and at the international level</u>. They convert these Bonds to investment securities and sell them at the international level.

CCA is the ticker on the Stock Exchange; they actually sell stock and shares on the New York Stock Exchange. CWX, CWD & CWG, when it goes to Frankfurt (CWG), when it goes to Berlin (CWDCCA Correction Corporation of America and they go international which means Berlin & Frankfurt Germany and they use a different Sticker Symbol. Who owns CCA? Don Russell, he owns 64 Million shares of it. John Ferguson, he's the vice president and owns about 35 Million shares. They are on the board of directors. There's another corporation called Dillon Corrections owned by David Dillon and what they did was they merged with Trinity Vender Investments and Dillon and they became SD Warburg and their located in Chicago Illinois and their hooked up with the EIS Bank which is the Bank of International Settlements located in Switzerland one of the largest banks in the world.

All this stuff is in that Treatise; there's a lot of information in that; you need to sit down and read that so you can understand what's going on before you do anything. **This is why people don't win in court; if you don't redeem the Bond**.... it's got the word Principal up there; you're the principal. Who is the Surety? Straw man is the Surety so you put the Straw man down as the Surety and you put yourself down as the Principal. Then you fill out a Performance Bond. The Performance Bond is the Reinsurance for the Bid Bond; put yourself down and the guarantor or reinsure. The Performance Bond is 274. You have 3 different Bonds: Bid Bond; Performance Bond & Payment Bond. The Payment Bond is the underwriter of the Performance Bond. You can do all three Bonds. You can underwrite the performance bond and underwrite the bid with the Performance Bond, that's the reinsure. **Their doing it for you because nobody knows this stuff**. You're the one that actually created all of this.
Always Demand for full settlement and closure; your running the account, you're the Fiduciary Trustee over the account – tell them what to do. You're the **Principal and owner of the account**, tell them what to do – tell them you want full settlement and closure of the account. You have to do this from the get-go. Here's the wording you use: I ACCEPT YOUR CHARGE(S) FOR VALUE AND CONSIDERATION [you have to use the words VALUE and CONSIDERATION] This is what I did...there's different forms that need to be used and that's VALUE & CONSIDERATION. I ACCEPT YOUR CHARGE FOR VALUE & CONSIDERATION IN RETURN FOR POST SETTLEMENT AND CLOSURE...OF ACCOUNT [put down your 9 digit social security number and put down CUSIP & AUTOTRIS No. AUTOTRIS means **Automated Tracking Identification System**.

Your social security number is the same as your **AUTOTRIS** numer. Don't put the dashes in there, just the 9 digit, that's the **CUSIP** When you say **CUSIP & AUTOTRIS** they know exactly what you're talking about. The **COMMITTEE ON UNIFORM SECURITIES IDENTIFICATION PROCESSES**. CUSIP is spelled C-U-S-I-P. Theirall listed in the Handbook called the Committee. **COMMITTEE ON UNIFORM SECURITIES IDENTIFICATION PROCESSES**. That's what CUSIP is. CUSIP uses your Social Security Number to identify you because the Birth Certificate is a Security...it is an investment security and they have all the original Birth Certificates which are registered at the State level with the Department of Human Recourses and then they go to the Department of Commerce and the Federal level and then to the DTC. The Depository Trust Corporation at 55 Water Street which has all the Birth Certificates registered. CUSIP is a Trade Mark of Standard & Poors. Who is Standard & Poors? Standard

& Poors is located underneath in the DTC building underneath 55 Water Street New York City.

Use the 9 digit number. for the Account, CUSIP & AUTOTRIS]. They use it for ICID too. What you do is put down Acceptance For Value and Consideration and Return for full Settlement and Closure of the Account [number] then put your account CUSIP # & AUTOTRIS # and put your social security number after that and then put down your case number.

I ACCEPT YOUR CHARGES FOR VALUE & CONSIDERATION IN RETURN AND POST SETTLMENT & CLOSURE [PUT CASE NUMBER] & AUTOTRIS & CUSIP ACCOUNT #& THEN PUT YOUR SOCIAL SECURITY # AFTER IT. Then DATE it and ENDORSE it. That comes after the AUTOTRIS & POST SETTLEMENT you say… "**PLEASE USE MY EXEMPTION FOR FULL SETTLEMENT & CLOSURE OF THIS ACCOUNT AS THIS ACCOUNT IS PRE-PAID AND EXEMPT FROM LEVY. UNDER RULE 8 OF THE FRCP, I ACCEPT THE CHARGES FOR VALUE & CONSIDERATION IN RETURN PLEASE USE MY EXEMPTION AS PRINCIPAL FOR POST SETTLEMENT & CLOSURE OF CASE NUMBER & CUSIP & AUTOTRIS ACCOUNT NUMBERS [SS #] AS THIS ACCOUNT IS PRE-PAID & EXEMPT FROM LEVY and you would date it and endorse it**. Date down here and endorse down here. This is how to pre-pay and exempt from levy then date it and endorse it. You have to endorse it as the Authorized Representative, your not going to assume liability. What they do is they put your AUTOTRIS number which is the AUTOMATED TRACKING IDENTIFICAITON SYSTEM; they put it in a Manuel…it's in a module and every Federal Agency and every State agency has your tracking number. They have it in the criminal task force that uses it and so do all of the courts and all of the police departments the City, County Sheriff, FEMA, HOMELAND SECURITY. They all use this.

Judges and lawyers don't understand commercial law. They do not teach commercial law at law school. **They have a special school for them and it's on a need to know basis**. No-one uses this stuff…the problem is no-one knows this. When you use commercial paper what does it mean? It means that you understand what your doing. The **law always assumes that you know…you were doing this since you were born** until you reach the age of accountability which is 18 years of age or what they call adulthood. Your considered an adult at 18 in some states [some states its 21] your responsible for your actions. The problem with this country is that no-one wants any responsibility. **If your holding yourself out and using commercial paper on a daily basis that legal definition makes you an expert or you wouldn't be using it so they presume that when you go into the courtroom you know all this . Ignorance of the Law is No Excuse.** If you don't show up incourt with an attorney…..this is why they drill you about competency; mental capacity because you go in there and start arguing with these people. When you're in a commercial setting, you don't want to argue with these people.

This is called a **Fiction-of-Law**; this comes out of Black's Law and what they are referring you to when you look up "**Fiction-of-Law**" is "**Legal Fiction**". Why do they call it "Legal Fiction"? OK, here's the definition of what a "**Legal Fiction**" is: Remember this is a "Fiction- of-Law". This is the reason why you can't go in there and argue, you're in a commercial court room, a commercial setting. *Now there's certain aspects of Admiralty where you can do that*. But when you're ina commercial setting, you cannot do that. Its says a "Legal Fiction": ***"The subject or something that may be true even though it may be untrue made especially into judicial reasoning to alter how a legal rule operates; specifically a devise by which a legal rule or institution is divergent from its original purpose to accomplish indirectly some other objects***. The constructive trust is an example of a legal fiction; also termed a "Fiction-of-Law". **Fictio Juris** is how they pronounce it. And they will not allow you to defeat this "Fiction-Of-Law". Why? Because this is what the **rules of decisions** that came out ofthe "**Erie v Thompkins**" decision and all of the courts at every level are using it…they're using **FICTIONS OF LAW**. Why? Because in **Admiralty Maritime Law** everything is **colorable**; it has the appearance of being real but is not real. *[Or as Howard Freeman put it: "Appears to be Genuine, but is not".]* ALL CLAIMS ARE TO BE GIVEN IN **COLOR** pleadings…I a **colorable claim**. And if you study Admiralty Maritime Law, that's all they talk about is **colorable claims**. How do you get color to a **pleading? Confession and Avoidance**. What is Confession and Avoidance? It's a Common Law Remedy. You **Confess**…what it is, you **confess that the Plaintiff has a Cause of action, but to Avoid the consequences of the action is by an** *Affirmative Defense*. *Confession and Avoidance* has been changed to **Rule 8** Federal Rules of Civil Procedure. What is an Affirmative Defense? The *Law Merchant*; the *Law of Principal & Equity*; The *Law of Discharge*; The *Law of Satisfaction: Bankruptcy*…are Affirmative Defenses? Are they Bankrupt? Sure they are. What you're trying to do is rebut the presumption, but you don't want to do that…what you want to do is go in there and settle the account as the Principal. Whenever they monetize debt, they always have a Principal from which they borrow all this money from.

Confession means you agree or accept; that's your commercial acceptance. "I ACCEPT THE CHARGE FOR VALUE AND CONSIDERATION AND RETURN AND FOR FULL SETTLEMENT FOR CASE AND ACCOUNT NUMBER. PLEASE USE MY EXEMPTION [If that is the correct ruling in these courts today it would be good to preclude that statement with…"Pursuant to Rule 8 FRCP "I Accept For Value". Now your giving the Judge the Rule under which you're doing the acceptance and now can't wiggle out and accept you're acceptance. **Rule 8 is for affirmative defense. Common Law Rule of confession and Avoidance under Affirmative Defenses**. They have to give you an out. Whenever you create a liability, you always have to create a remedy. Every liability has a Remedy attached to it and Affirmative Defenses under Rule 8 is your Remedy from every commercial liability. What do I mean when I say these are "Pre-Paid Accounts"? What they do when the industrial society borrows money to manufacture product like when GMC manufactures automobiles, they borrow all money to manufacture these automobiles. They're on the **Public side of the accounting ledger**. What do I mean by Public side? Everything over here is private and everything over there is Public. This is where the principal is and that is where the Debtors are. Your straw man is over on the Public side he's on the AUTOTRIS side and when your   over   on   his   side   your   in   the   Public…your   in   Bankruptcy.

what is a stock warrant

Q All News Videos Shopping Images More   Tools

About 67,200,000 results (0.66 seconds)

View all

A **stock warrant** represents the right to purchase a company's **stock** at a specific price and at a specific date. A **stock warrant** is issued directly by a company to an investor. ... **Stock** options are typically traded between investors. A **stock warrant** represents future capital for a company.

https://www.investopedia.com › ask › stock-option-warrant

Stock Warrants vs. Stock Options: What's the Difference?

     You're the **Principal and the owner**. **You're the Stockholder**…you're the Bank. This is not my opinion, this is what's going on…I'll take you in any bank…I own my own bank. [Private Banker: Black Law 6th] I draw up my own charges. Ya, you're the lien holder. *Holder-in-due-course; stockowner, owner and the principal; you own the preferred stock and the common stock*. This is where the principal is. The straw man is the beneficiary…they cannot run…you're the bridge between the private and the public side [as are Notaries]. What is? Your exemption is that's why they give you your exemption. This is the debits and this is the credits. **Credits are liabilities and debits are assets**. they can't pass it from the credit side to the debit side because they are constantly in Dishonor. Debits are private and credits are public. *Most people are floundering around on the Public side of the accounting ledger*. They're borrowing all of this money using your credit, but your responsible for the straw man. Who do they charge when you come into the court room? Whose name is on the complaint? Straw man! Their charging him aren't they? Is he liable? Sure he is. *So he has to pay doesn't he*? So if he doesn't pay what happens? **YOU PAY FOR HIM AS YOU ASSUME THE RESPONSIBILITY OF THE FIDUCIARY TRUSTEE SO THEY PUT YOU IN PRISON AND SELL YOUR ACCOUNT**. All they have to do is create a presumption, remember it's all colorable and what does colorable mean…its not real. So do they have to have a **real complaint**? No. Do they have to have a **real warrant**? No. What did I just read to you about "Fiction-of-Law"? And they will not allow you to overcome this. What they do is if you go in there and start arguing with these people about jurisdiction or "I don't owe this" or "That's not my name" or "I'm not going to give you my name"; your going to be found in contempt.

You are the Creditor. What does a creditor do…a creditor pays his debts…you're the only one that's got any money. The banks don't have any money…everyone on the public side is bankrupt. That's why they had to create the straw man so that they would have a remedy. Do Not go in there and argue with the judge. "I DON'T SPELL MY NAME IN ALL CAPITAL LETTERS". They'll appoint counsel for you…what you do is a "**LETTER OF ROGATORY**" Its called a "Letter of Rogatory" [what's that mean] A **letter of Advice**. What do you put into this "Letter of Rogatory"?   You instruct the Attorney that you are doing an "**Acceptance for Honor**" and you want an accounting of the total amount of the Bill of the full settlement and closure of the account then you give your CUSIP and AUTOTIS number and your case number…you want to know what the total amount of the Bill is post settlement and closure of this account. What you want to do ….they can't talk to you for the simple reason they don't understand commercial law Give them a "Letter Rogatory". This is a letter of advice, this is out of "Clerk's Praxis" page 80. What you say in the letter is …put your name in here and put "**I appoint…put your Judge's name here and you write "I appoint JUDGE JOE BLOW as my fiduciary trustee…case number and AUTOTRIS and CUSIP [SS NO.] AND USE MY EXEMPTION AS PRINCIPAL FOR FULL SETTLEMENT AND CLOSURE OF THIS CASE AND ACCOUNT and Date it and endorse it.** You're actually creating all the money for the Bank…their using your money and going out and making depravities and fractionalizing making Trillions of dollars off you and everyone asks me if this stuff works. We need a reality check. we issued an International Bill of Exchange to an APO adult parole officer and they dissolved the case.

What you demand always is the Bond. **The Bid Bond, Performance Bond & Payment Bond.**, I'm the principal, I want my capital and interest back.. The reason why you have to use an **International Bill of Exchange** is that December 8, 1988 the UnitedStates became a party to [**UNICITROL this acronym is not correct**] convention. The "**War Powers**" are of the Executive Branch and anytime you're under the **War Powers Act and with the Trading with the Enemy**, you're subject to "**Catcher" & "Seizure"** wherever they find you. The Bond is the key to this ….the Bond I'm talking about is the **Bid Bond**. There's two sets of Bonds…there's GSA 24 (General Services Administration). It's called ….SF means Standard Form [comment]…these are GSA Form Numbers….these are Federal Forms. There are two sets of Federal Forms. The GSA SF24, that's your "**Bid Bond**",: GSA SF25 is your "**Performance Bond**": and the GSA SF25A is the "**Payment Bond**". [Question: something about the UNCITROL Treaty] The United States became a party to the UNCITROL convention in December 8th 1988 and it supercedes Article III of the UCC…

This is the **Bid Bond**; this is the **Performance Bond** & this is the **Payment Bond**. This is the Reinsurance here…the Performance Bond is the Reinsurance. The Payment Bond is the Underwriter. Do you know how they do it in Admiralty? They write your name under the name of someone else and that's called the underwriter its all done with a signature. All Bonds are insurance…its all Admiralty. Well they usually have seals…all insurance companies have seals. Make a seal on it…make your own seal on it. If you're the Principal do you have to have somebody tell you what to do? If you're the Creditor then start acting like one. How does the

Creditor act? Does he go after the Debt or the money? They come after you don't they? What's good for the goose is good for the gander [question] Yes; they guarantee the payment of the Bid Bond. The Payment Bond is the Underwriter. They get an <u>Investment Broker</u> and an <u>Investment Banker</u> to underwrite these Bonds. The Performance Bond guarantees the Bid Bond. Either the Insurance company or the Broker underwrites the Performance Bond. If you go into the Websites I gave you, US Distcourts, you'll see a whole list of admitted reinsures and listed Sureties…t

HOW TO FILE FOR A BANKERS EIN NUMBER

1. Organizational Type:

2. The "LEGAL NAME"

3. The Trade name is the ALL CAPS NAME, Private Bank E & T

4. The county you live in

5. Start Date: Date of Application

6. Physical Address:

7. Physical Location:

8. Responsible party: the ALL CAPS NAME

9. SSN:

10. Principle Business Activity? Other Banking/Asset Management

11. Principle Product:? PRIVATE UNINCORPORATED BANK

12. Additional: Non-Profit Tax Exempt Organization

13. Reason For Applying? Starting a new business

    *Make sure you copy the document because the IRS won't send it to you! When it say's, "Do you want a pdf?" say "Yes" – 82 number.

Apply for this number at IRS.gov & use it in lieu of an ssn when opening a bank account.
FIRST MIDDLE LAST NAME PRIVATE BANK E&T

the E&T is for Estate & Trust

Form **56**
(Rev. December 2019)
Department of the Treasury
Internal Revenue Service

Notice Concerning Fiduciary Relationship
(Internal Revenue Code Sections 6036 and 6903)

▶ Go to *www.irs.gov/Form56* for instructions and the latest information.

OMB No. 1545-0013

Part I — Identification

Name of person for whom you are acting (as shown on the tax return)

Identifying number

Decedent's social security no.

Address of person for whom you are acting (number, street, and room or suite no.)

City or town, state, and ZIP code (If a foreign address, see instructions.)

Fiduciary's name

Address of fiduciary (number, street, and room or suite no.)

City or town, state, and ZIP code

Telephone number (optional)
( )

Section A. Authority

1 Authority for fiduciary relationship. Check applicable box:
  a ☐ Court appointment of testate estate (valid will exists)
  b ☐ Court appointment of intestate estate (no valid will exists)
  c ☐ Court appointment as guardian or conservator
  d ☐ Fiduciary of intestate estate
  e ☐ Valid trust instrument and amendments
  f ☐ Bankruptcy or assignment for the benefit or creditors
  g ☐ Other. Describe ▶
2a If box 1a, 1b, or 1d is checked, enter the date of death ▶
  b If box 1c, 1e, 1f, or 1g is checked, enter the date of appointment, taking office, or assignment or transfer of assets ▶

Section B. Nature of Liability and Tax Notices

3 Type of taxes (check all that apply): ☐ Income ☐ Gift ☐ Estate ☐ Generation-skipping transfer ☐ Employment
  ☐ Excise ☐ Other (describe) ▶

4 Federal tax form number (check all that apply): a ☐ 706 series b ☐ 709 c ☐ 940 d ☐ 941, 943, 944
  e ☐ 1040 or 1040-SR f ☐ 1041 g ☐ 1120 h ☐ Other (list) ▶

5 If your authority as a fiduciary does not cover all years or tax periods, check here . . . . ▶ ☐
  and list the specific years or periods ▶

For Paperwork Reduction Act and Privacy Act Notice, see separate instructions.   Cat. No. 16375I   Form **56** (Rev. 12-2019)

Form 56 (Rev. 12-2019) Page **2**

Part II — Revocation or Termination of Notice

Section A—Total Revocation or Termination

6 Check this box if you are revoking or terminating all prior notices concerning fiduciary relationships on file with the Internal Revenue Service for the same tax matters and years or periods covered by this notice concerning fiduciary relationship ▶ ☐
Reason for termination of fiduciary relationship. Check applicable box:
- **a** ☐ Court order revoking fiduciary authority
- **b** ☐ Certificate of dissolution or termination of a business entity
- **c** ☐ Other. Describe ▶ _____

Section B—Partial Revocation

7a Check this box if you are revoking earlier notices concerning fiduciary relationships on file with the Internal Revenue Service for the same tax matters and years or periods covered by this notice concerning fiduciary relationship . . . . ▶ ☐
b Specify to whom granted, date, and address, including ZIP code.
▶ _____

Section C—Substitute Fiduciary

8 Check this box if a new fiduciary or fiduciaries have been or will be substituted for the revoking or terminating fiduciary and specify the name(s) and address(es), including ZIP code(s), of the new fiduciary(ies) . . . . ▶ ☐
▶ _____

Part III — Court and Administrative Proceedings

Name of court (if other than a court proceeding, identify the type of proceeding and name of agency)			Date proceeding initiated		
Address of court			Docket number of proceeding		
City or town, state, and ZIP code		Date	Time	☐ a.m. ☐ p.m.	Place of other proceedings

Part IV — Signature

Please Sign Here
Under penalties of perjury, I declare that I have examined this document, including any accompanying statements, and to the best of my knowledge and belief, it is true, correct, and complete.

▶ _____ _____ _____
  Fiduciary's signature   Title, if applicable   Date

Form **56** (Rev. 12-2019)

Form **W-8BEN**
(Rev. February 2006)
Department of the Treasury
Internal Revenue Service

Certificate of Foreign Status of Beneficial Owner for United States Tax Withholding

▶ Section references are to the Internal Revenue Code.   ▶ See separate instructions.
▶ Give this form to the withholding agent or payer. Do not send to the IRS.

OMB No. 1545-1621

Do not use this form for:	Instead, use Form:
• A U.S. citizen or other U.S. person, including a resident alien individual	W-9
• A person claiming that income is effectively connected with the conduct of a trade or business in the United States	W-8ECI
• A foreign partnership, a foreign simple trust, or a foreign grantor trust (see instructions for exceptions)	W-8ECI or W-8IMY
• A foreign government, international organization, foreign central bank of issue, foreign tax-exempt organization, foreign private foundation, or government of a U.S. possession that received effectively connected income or that is claiming the applicability of section(s) 115(2), 501(c), 892, 895, or 1443(b) (see instructions)	W-8ECI or W-8EXP

Note: *These entities should use Form W-8BEN if they are claiming treaty benefits or are providing the form only to claim they are a foreign person exempt from backup withholding.*

• A person acting as an intermediary W-8IMY

Note: *See instructions for additional exceptions.*

Part I Identification of Beneficial Owner (See instructions.)

1 Name of individual or organization that is the beneficial owner	2 Country of incorporation or organization

3 Type of beneficial owner: ☐ Individual   ☐ Corporation   ☐ Disregarded entity   ☐ Partnership   ☐ Simple trust
☐ Grantor trust   ☐ Complex trust   ☐ Estate   ☐ Government   ☐ International organization
☐ Central bank of issue   ☐ Tax-exempt organization   ☐ Private foundation

4 Permanent residence address (street, apt. or suite no., or rural route). **Do not use a P.O. box or in-care-of address.**

City or town, state or province. Include postal code where appropriate.	Country (do not abbreviate)

5 Mailing address (if different from above)

City or town, state or province. Include postal code where appropriate.	Country (do not abbreviate)

6 U.S. taxpayer identification number, if required (see instructions) ☐ SSN or ITIN ☐ EIN	7 Foreign tax identifying number, if any (optional)

8 Reference number(s) (see instructions)

Part II Claim of Tax Treaty Benefits (if applicable)

9 I certify that (check all that apply):

a ☐ The beneficial owner is a resident of .... within the meaning of the income tax treaty between the United States and that country.

b ☐ If required, the U.S. taxpayer identification number is stated on line 6 (see instructions).

c ☐ The beneficial owner is not an individual, derives the item (or items) of income for which the treaty benefits are claimed, and, if applicable, meets the requirements of the treaty provision dealing with limitation on benefits (see instructions).

d ☐ The beneficial owner is not an individual, is claiming treaty benefits for dividends received from a foreign corporation or interest from a U.S. trade or business of a foreign corporation, and meets qualified resident status (see instructions).

e ☐ The beneficial owner is related to the person obligated to pay the income within the meaning of section 267(b) or 707(b), and will file Form 8833 if the amount subject to withholding received during a calendar year exceeds, in the aggregate, $500,000.

10 Special rates and conditions (if applicable—see instructions): The beneficial owner is claiming the provisions of Article .... of the treaty identified on line 9a above to claim a .... % rate of withholding on (specify type of income): ....
Explain the reasons the beneficial owner meets the terms of the treaty article: --

Part III Notional Principal Contracts

11 ☐ I have provided or will provide a statement that identifies those notional principal contracts from which the income is **not** effectively connected with the conduct of a trade or business in the United States. I agree to update this statement as required.

Part IV Certification

Under penalties of perjury, I declare that I have examined the information on this form and to the best of my knowledge and belief it is true, correct, and complete. I further certify under penalties of perjury that:
1 I am the beneficial owner (or am authorized to sign for the beneficial owner) of all the income to which this form relates,
2 The beneficial owner is not a U.S. person,
3 The income to which this form relates is (a) not effectively connected with the conduct of a trade or business in the United States, (b) effectively connected but is not subject to tax under an income tax treaty, or (c) the partner's share of a partnership's effectively connected income, **and**
4 For broker transactions or barter exchanges, the beneficial owner is an exempt foreign person as defined in the instructions.
Furthermore, I authorize this form to be provided to any withholding agent that has control, receipt, or custody of the income of which I am the beneficial owner or any withholding agent that can disburse or make payments of the income of which I am the beneficial owner.

Sign Here ▶ _____   _____   _____
Signature of beneficial owner (or individual authorized to sign for beneficial owner)   Date (MM-DD-YYYY)   Capacity in which acting

For Paperwork Reduction Act Notice, see separate instructions.   Cat. No. 25047Z   Form **W-8BEN** (Rev. 2-2006)

Printed on Recycled Paper

Affidavit of Foreign Status

Certified Mail Number: _____

Date: _____

Jeffery Wayne McBride Jr,
c/o 1101 E Cumberland Ave Ste 201H-108
Tampa, Florida [33602]
Republic United States
zip code exempt (DMM 122.32)

FOREIGN STATUS AFFIDAVIT
National But Not Citizen Per 8 USC 1408

FLORIDA /REPUBLIC   )
)   Subscribed, Sworn and Sealed
TAMPA   )

PREAMBLE

The following Affidavit of Foreign Status is a public notice to all interested parties concerning the Affiant's "birthrights" and his "status" as an "AMERICAN INHABITANT", as that status would apply with respect to the American States (the 50 independent States of the Union) and also with respect to the "United States", as follows:

1. The Affiant, Jeffery Wayne McBride Jr , , was natural born a freeSovereign in Illinois , which is one of the sovereign States of the Union of several States joined together to comprise the confederation known as the united States of America. He is, therefore, a "nonresident alien" individual with respect to the "United States", which entity obtains its exclusive legislative authority and jurisdiction from Article 1, Section 8, Clause 17

and Article 4, Section 3, Clause 2 of the Constitution for the united States of America. The Affiant's parents were Sovereigns also, born in sovereign States of the Union. As the progeny of Sovereign people, the Affiant was born "... one of the sovereign people .... A constituent member of the sovereignty synonymous with the people." Scott vs Sanford, 19 How. 404. The Affiant is alien to so-called 14th Amendment "United States" citizenship, and also nonresident to so-called 14th Amendment State residency, and therefore he is a "nonresident alien" with respect to both. As a Sovereign whose Citizenship originated in Illinois by birth, and who has remained intact in Florida since the year , the Affiant is also a foreigner (alien) with respect to the other 49 2019 States of the Union and with respect to the "United States". As a consequence of his birth, the Affiant is an "American Inhabitant". And further

2. The Affiant, to the best of his informed knowledge, has not entered into any valid agreements of "voluntary servitude". And further

3. The Affiant is a "NONRESIDENT ALIEN" with respect to the "United States", as that term is defined and used within the Internal Revenue Code (Title 26, United State Code) and/or Title 27 and the rules and regulations promulgated thereunder as follows:

The Internal Revenue Code (Title 26, United State Code) and associated federal regulations, clearly and thoroughly make provision for Americans born and living within one of the 50 Sovereign States of America, to wit:

Section 1.871-4 Proof of residence of aliens.

(a) Rules of evidence. The following rules of evidence shall govern in determining whether or not an alien within the United States has acquired residence therein for purposes of the income tax.

(b) Nonresidence presumed. An alien by reason of his alienage, is presumed to be a nonresident alien.

[26 CFR 1.871-4]

And further

4. The Affiant was not born or naturalized in the "United States", consequently he is not a "citizen of the "United States" nor a "United States citizen", as those terms are defined and used within the Internal Revenue Code (26 U.S.C.) and/or Title 27 and the rules and regulations promulgated thereunder; and, therefore, he is not subject to the limited, exclusive territorial or political jurisdiction and authority of the "United States" as defined.

The "United States" is definitive and specific when it defines one of its citizens, as follows:

Section 1.1-1

(c) Who is a citizen. Every person born or naturalized in the United States and subject to its jurisdiction is a citizen.
[26 CFR 1.1-1(c)]

And further

5. The Affiant is not a "citizen of the United States" nor a "United States citizen living abroad", as those phrases are defined and used in the Internal Revenue Code (26 U.S.C.) and/or Title 27 and the rules and regulations promulgated thereunder.
And further

6. The Affiant is not a "resident alien residing within the geographical boundaries of the United States", as that phrase is defined and used in the Internal Revenue Code (26 U.S.C.) and/or Title 27 and the rules and regulations promulgated thereunder. And further

7. The Affiant is not a "United States person", a "domestic corporation", "estate", "trust", "fiduciary" or "partnership" as those terms are defined and used within the Internal Revenue Code (26 U.S.C.) and/or Title 27 and the rules

and regulations promulgated thereunder. And further

8. The Affiant is not an "officer", "employee" or "elected official" of the "United States", of a "State" or of any political subdivision thereof, nor of the District of Columbia, nor of any agency or instrumentality of one or more of the foregoing, nor an "officer" of a "United States corporation", as those terms are defined and used within the Internal Revenue Code (26 U.S.C.) and/or Title 27 and the rules and regulations promulgated thereunder. And further

9. The Affiant receives no "income" or "wages with respect to employment" from any sources within the territorial jurisdiction of the "United States" and does not have an "office or other fixed place of business" within the "United States" from which the Affiant derives any "income" or "wages" as such, as those terms and phrases are used and defined within the Internal Revenue Code (26 U.S.C.) and/or Title 27 and the rules and regulations promulgated thereunder. And further

10. The Affiant has never engaged in the conduct of a "trade or business" within the "United States", nor does the Affiant receive any income or other remuneration effectively connected with the conduct of a "trade or business" within the "United States", as those terms are defined and used within the Internal Revenue Code (26 U.S.C.) and/or Title 27 and the rules and regulations promulgated thereunder. And further

11. The Affiant receives no "income", "wages", "self-employment income" or "other remuneration" from sources within the "United States", as those terms are defined and used in the Internal Revenue Code (26 U.S.C.) and/or Title 27 and the rules and regulations promulgated thereunder. All remuneration paid to the Affiant is for services rendered outside (without) the exclusive territorial, political and legislative jurisdiction and authority of the "United States". And further

12. The Affiant has never had an "office" or "place of business" within the "United States", as those terms are defined and used in the Internal Revenue Code (26 U.S.C.) and/or Title 27 and the rules and regulations promulgated thereunder. And further

13. The Affiant has never been a "United States employer", nor "employer", nor "employee" which also includes but is not limited to an "employee" and/or "employer" for a "United States" "household", and/or "agricultural" activity, as those terms are defined and used in the Internal Revenue Code (26 U.S.C.) and/or Title 27 and the rules and regulations promulgated thereunder. And further

14. The Affiant has never been involved in any "commerce" within the territorial jurisdiction of the "United States" which also includes but is not limited to "alcohol", "tobacco" and "firearms" and Title 26, Subtitle D and E excises and privileged occupations, as those terms are defined and used in the Internal Revenue Code (26 U.S.C.) and/or Title 27 and the rules and regulations promulgated thereunder. And further

15. The Affiant has never been a "United States" "withholding agent" as those terms are defined and used in the Internal Revenue Code (26 U.S.C.) and/or Title 27 and the rules and regulations promulgated thereunder. And further

16. The Affiant had no liability for any type, kind or class of Federal Income Tax in past years, and was and is entitled to a full and complete refund of any amounts withheld, because any liability asserted and amounts withheld were premised upon a mutual mistake of fact regarding the Affiant's status. The Affiant has never knowingly, intentionally, and voluntarily changed his Citizenship status nor has he ever knowingly, intentionally, and voluntarily elected to be treated as a "resident" of the "United States". And further

17. The Affiant, to the best of his current knowledge, owes no "tax" of any type, class or kind to the "United States" as those terms are defined and used in the Internal Revenue Code (26 U.S.C.) and/or Title 27 and the rules and regulations promulgated thereunder. And further

18. The Affiant anticipates no liability for any type, class or kind of federal income tax in the current year, because the Affiant does not intend to reside in the "United States", he does not intend to be treated as either a "resident" or a "citizen" of the "United States", he is not and does not intend to be involved in the conduct of any "trade or business" within

the "United States" or receive any "income" or "wages" from sources within the "United States", as those terms are defined and used in the Internal Revenue Code (26 U.S.C.) and/or Title 27 and the rules and regulations promulgated thereunder. And further

19. The Affiant, by means of knowingly intelligent acts done with sufficient awareness of the relevant circumstances and consequences (Brady vs U.S., 397 U.S. 742, 748 (1970)) never agreed or consented to be given a federal Social Security Number (SSN), same said as to a federal Employee Identification Number (EIN) and, therefore, waives and releases from liability the "United States" and any State of the Union of 50 States, for any present or future benefits that the Affiant may be entitled to claim under the Old-Age Survivors and the Disability Insurance Act, and/or the Federal Unemployment Tax Act. Additionally, your Affiant makes no claim to any present or future benefits under any of the foregoing; and

20. Therefore, I, Jeffery Wayne McBride Jr , , am a natural born freeinhabitant and, as such, a Sovereign Citizen/Principal inhabiting the California Republic. Therefore, I am not "within the United States" but lawfully I am "without the United States" (per Title 28, U.S.C., Section 1746, Subsection 1), and therefore I have no standing capacity to sign any tax form which displays the perjury clause pursuant to Title 28, Section 1746, Subsection 2. And further

PLEASE NOTE WELL: At no time will the Affiant construe any of the foregoing terms defined within the Internal Revenue Code, Title 26, United State Code, or within any of the other United State Code, in a metaphorical sense. When terms are not words of art and are explicitly defined within the Code and/or within a Statute, the Affiant relies at all times upon the clear language of the terms as they are defined therein, NO MORE and NO LESS:

... When aid to construction of the meaning of words, as used in the statute, is available, there certainly can be no 'rule of law' which forbids its use, however clear the words may appear on 'superficial examination' ....

[United States vs American Trucking Association]
[310 U.S. 534, 543,544 (1939)]

This unsworn certification is being executed WITHOUT the "United States", pursuant to Section 1746(1) of Title 28, United State Code, Federal Rules of Civil Procedure:

I affirm under penalty of perjury, under the laws of the United States of America, that I executed the foregoing for the purposes and considerations herein expressed, in the capacity stated, and that the statements contained herein are true and correct, to the best of my knowledge.

Executed Anno Domini, on this the_____day in the month of

, 2021.

Subscribed, sealed and affirmed to this_____day of

, 2021.

Jeffery Wayne McBride Jr , , Citizen/Principal, by special Appearance, in PropriaPersona, proceeding Sui Juris, with Assistance, Special, with explicit reservation of all of my unalienable rights and without prejudice to any of my unalienable rights.

Jeffery Wayne McBride Jr,
c/o 1101 E Cumberland Ave Ste 201H-108
Tampa, Florida [33602]
RepublicUnited States
zip code exempt (DMM 122.32)

Georgia All-Purpose Acknowledgement

GEORGIA STATE/REPUBLIC   )
)
COUNTY OF _____   )

On the_____day of_____, 2021 Anno Domini, before me personally appeared Jeffery Wayne McBride Jr , , personally known to me(or proved to me on the basis of satisfactory evidence) to be the Person whose name is subscribed to the within instrument and acknowledged to me that he executed the same in His authorized capacity, and that by His signature on this instrument the Person, or the entity upon behalf of which the Person acted, executed the instrument. Purpose of Notary Public is for identification only, and not for entrance into any foreign jurisdiction.

WITNESS my hand and official seal.

_____
Notary Public

CASE NUMBER: 21CP200858
EXHIBIT 121212

LETTER ROGATORY FOR RELIEF

Under the Hague Convention Title 18 §1781

I, : **Jeffery W- of The Family:McBride**, a living Soul and breathing Man and Executor for the **JEFFERY WAYNE MCBRIDE JR** Cestui que trust, notice the Court of my Letter Rogatory to the **FULTON COUNTY, GEORGIA COURTS** and demand my name be cleared of this alleged family court case for the reasons set forth below:

1) I, : **Jeffery W- of The Family:McBride**,, have learned that this alleged Court that has scheduled a case/cause/claim against me is not really a court as per the Constitution of the United States of America (not an Article III Court), but rather a military tribunal under Admiralty jurisdiction and is operated as a private, for profit corporation listed on Dun and Bradstreet.

2) I have learned of the fraud that goes on behind the scenes of these alleged criminal cases, which are really civil claims in equity, and the steps taken to securitize these civil claims, without giving full disclosure to the people. I am hereby letting the court know that I am opting out of any contract and do not allow any documents regarding me or my cestui que trust to be securitized and sold to any investors etc.

3) As you may be fully aware, the fraudulent process is as follows: All cases are civil, though often fraudulently called criminal. The courts are operating under trust law, assuming the Defendant and Respondent is a decedent (civiliter mortus). After finding the alleged Defendant guilty, the court clerks sell the judgments to the Federal Courts. Since the Defendant and or Respondent is a decedent, presumed to be a ward of the court, incompetent and of unsound mind, the court officials consider themselves as a beneficiary as the powers that be (international bankers) have concocted a reverse trust scheme on we, the people, who are supposed to be the beneficiaries because we are the actual creditors.

4) When a judge asks if a person understands, he/she is asking if the person is liable for the bond. I am not responsible for the bond of this/these cases, but I will appoint the Judge as Trustee/Fiduciary and be the beneficiary of all proceeds.

5) The judgments are stamped with something to the effect of Pay To The Order Of__ on the back and taken to the federal discount window. The judgment now becomes a note

6) The notes are then pooled together and then become securities, which are yet pooled together and sold as bonds.

7) Said bonds are liens against me, a defendant-in-error.

8) The United States Attorney's Office has a put code number, NAICS (North American Identification Security Classification. Said NAICS number enables the United States Attorney's Office to trade globally all securities.

9) All US federal courts are registered with the DOD (Department of Defense), where they are registered with CCR (Contractor's Central Registration), under the DOD, which another department called DLIS (Defense Logistics Information Service), which issues a cage code, which means a commercial and government entity, which everything corresponds with their bank account.

10) Said United States Attorney's Office and Courts have a Duns number (Dun & Bradstreet).

11) Everything filed into court is securitized without the knowledge or consent of the people or of all parties involved.

12) All criminal cases not heard in an Article 3 court (District Court of the United States) are actually civil; however, the courts again commit fraud by labeling the case as criminal, even for an infraction as minimal as a parking ticket. All cases which are plead out or have a guilty conviction label the civil defendants (through unlawful conversion) as felons when they are not. This is fraud upon the people at large, and certainly fraud upon the alleged Defendants-in-error.

13) The Bank Account is at Federal Reserve Bank of New York, in New York City. The Depository Agreement is signed by the Clerk of Court.

14) All securities are then deposited with the DTC in New York.

15) An Escrow Agent is used as a go-between - between the Clerk's Office and the Federal Reserve Bank of New York.

16) The securities end up being listed through the Seventh Circuit (Chicago, IL), then sent to the DTCC, the clearinghouse whom lists the securities for trading.

17) All of the lawyers involved are acting as private debt collectors according to the **FDCPA (Title 15§1692).** The BAR Association exempts them from having to be registered as such; however, they operate through call warrants, which are like a put, or a call. Doing margin calls is where they convert a case through (similar to a Writ of Execution) use the case number to buy equity securities.

18) Everything filed into court is securitized and turned into negotiable instruments, and then turning them into securities. These items are sold commercial items, calling them distress debts (Unifund). The items are then pooled together in what is now called a hedge fund, where they are sold globally.

19) Anytime when there is risk management involved, it is for the securities. This is an underwriting company. When the hedge funds are going into the global market, they go through Luer Hermes, a bond holder and underwriting company and subdivision of Alliance SE, of Munich ,Germany (Pimco Bonds).

20) After 9 months, all paper is converted to a securities status. This is defined in **Title 15§77(a)(b)(1)** and an now considered to be an investment contract. The paper is endorsed to become a security, and the trust is then collapsed.

21) The courts have an account with the IMF (International Monetary Fund) under Interpol. The Judges involved and the US Attorneys involved do not have an accessible Oath of Office , because they cover up the fact that the oath of office is between them and the IMF.

CASE NUMBER: 21CP200858
EXHIBIT 121212

22) The US Judges and US Attorneys are actually employees of the IMF and have expatriated out of the United States. They are now unregistered foreign agents under **Title 22**, which states all foreign agents must be registered. These hypocrites don't even adhere to their own codes.

23) The court judgments are deposited with the IMF. Since this case obviously involves me, I have a drawing s to all proceeds. See **UCC §3-305 and §3-306**. The court judgments are monopolized according to **Title 16**, which is a violation of anti-trust laws, and also unfair trade practices.

24) Indictments are True Bills, meaning they are negotiable instruments. The District Attorney failed to give me a 1099 OID showing me as the recipient of the funds, which is a fraud upon me. In my case, I have not been indicted, but still request a 1099 OID, unless the court wishes to close this account.

25) The unlawful funds, through fraud and deception, are deposited in the Federal Reserve Bank of New York and they have not paid the tax on this income. According to the IRC, this is a **§7201** of **Title 26** violation (willful failure to file with the intent to evade the tax).

26) A copy of the Depository Resolution Agreement was not made available to me from the Clerk of Court. The Clerk of Court makes deposits into the Federal Reserve Bank of New York via electronic funds transfers (EFT's).

27) The Clerk has a PMIA (Private Money Investment Account) is, which also has a government code. According to Clerks Praxis, the Clerk of the US District Court is the Registrar in Admiralty.

28) According to the **IRS §6209** Decoding Manual and the ADP (Automated Data Processing Manual), all 1099's are Class 5 gift and estate taxes. I am asking for a 1099 OID in this case, as I am not willing to gift you the proceeds. I am hereby asking for the proceeds in their entirety, including interest.

29) It is presumed that by the creation of the birth certificate my body and the labor therefrom is pledged to the State. This is patently absurd as this unilateral, quasi-contract is lacking in full disclosure to the parents and the babies still in their cribs.I have never pledged my rights nor my body, any labor thereof, nor any creation therefrom to any gifting program, including any court or court process.

30) I am not a charitable organization. I demand all funds from the cases (current and past cases) be sent to me within 30 days or I will file complaints to the IRS and SEC explaining the fraud and theft committed upon me, and issue a 1099 OID.

31) I demand my name and my cestui que trust name, **JEFFERY WAYNE MCBRIDE JR** be removed from any and all government databases indicating bad credit, commercial liens and/or the titles of criminal, felon and/or debtor be removed immediately and permanently NUNC PRO TUNC.

32) I hereby request a copy of the Depository Resolution Agreement from the Clerk of Court. And a W-9 from the Judge and the US Attorney involved, if you wish to proceed with this case.

33) I hereby notice the Court that I am the Executor of the cestui que trust of **JEFFERY WAYNE MCBRIDE JR**. According to **Title 26 §303 & §7701**, companies, corporations, and associations and trusts are all decedents. This means my all capital letters name is a legal estate. My all capital letters name falls into this class. I direct all of the affairs and financial affairs of **JEFFERY WAYNE MCBRIDE JR**, an Estate.

CASE NUMBER: 21CP200858
EXHIBIT 121212

34) I demand this case/account be closed and no further steps taken to securitize it.

35) I hereby ask the Court, as my fiduciary and trustee, to notify local agents and agencies to put me on a do not disturb or detain list so that we do not have to go through this again. Additionally, I demand compensation from the **FULTON COUNTY, GEORGIA** in the amount of **$50,000.00** for the commercial injury I have sustained from the loss of my property, loss of time from working, the cost of certified mailings of **AFFIDAVITS, NOTICE AND DEMAND** letters to the parties involved, the cost of filings and recordings as well as the expenses incurred for traveling as a result of being deprived of the use of my private property (automobile) which was unlawfully converted for public use.

36) I want to remain confident that the Court and its officers want to follow the law, and perhaps were unaware of the processes of civil and criminal cases and that the public policy enforcers are ignorant of the aforementioned facts regarding their often erroneous administration of the Cestui que trust.

37) I expect no further harassment from rogue unregistered foreign agents and public policy enforcers acting under color of law.

LETTER ROGATORY FOR RELIEF

FURTHER AFFIANT SAITH NOT.
Subscribed and sworn, without prejudice, and with all rights reserved,
(Printed Name:) :**JEFFERY W:** of the family name :**MCBRIDE JR**
Principal, by Special Appearance, proceeding Sui Juris.

Signed:_____
Date:_____

On this _____ day of _____, _____, before me, the undersigned, a Notary Public in and for _____, personally appeared the above-signed, known to me to be the one whose name is signed on this instrument, and has acknowledged to me that s/he has executed the same.

Signed:_____
Printed Name:_____
Date:_____
Address:_____

TRUST NUMBER: 21CP200858
EXHIBIT 3333

NOTICE OF MISTAKE

1. **TAKE NOTICE THAT:** In the matter of **SURETY** for the **JEFFERY WAYNE MCBRIDE JR** trust I believe that there has been a **MISTAKE**, as the **SOLE BENEFICIARY OF A PUBLIC DOCUMENT** has **been INCORRECTLY IDENTIFIED** as an "accused" and/or a "suspect".

2. **FORGIVE ME:** If I, **AND/OR PERSONS AND/OR FRIENDS OF THE COURT AND/OSUCH OTHER PARTIES ACTING IN MY INTERESTS,** have led **A COURT** and/or **STATUTORY BODY** and/or **A GOVERNMENT SERVICE** and/or **AGENTS** and/or **OFFICERS** of such bodies, to believe, by responding to "You", and/or "**JEFFERY WAYNE MCBRIDE JR**", and/or **SUCH OTHER IDENTIFICATION**, such bodies **HAVE ADDRESSED ME AS**, that I am the **PARTY WITH SURETY** in this matter, then that would be a **MISTAKE**, and please forgive me.

3. If I, **AND/OR PERSONS AND/OR FRIENDS OF THE COURT AND/OR SUCH OTHER PARTIES ACTING IN MY INTERESTS,** have led **A COURT** and/or **STATUTORY BODY** and/or A **GOVERNMENT SERVICE** and/or **AGENTS** and/or **OFFICERS** of such bodies, to believe, by responding to "You", and/or "**ATIF TATE** and/or **SUCH OTHER IDENTIFICATION**, such bodies **HAVE ADDRESSED ME AS**, that I am, in **ANY CAPACITY**, a *Pro Se* litigant and/or a **LEGAL PERSON** in this matter, then that would be a **MISTAKE**, as I **DO NOT CONSENT and WAIVE THE BENEFIT** to such titles (Waiver of the **CHANGE OF NAMES ACT OF FEDERAL RULES**), and please forgive me.

4. **THEREFORE:** As I have no knowledge of who "You" and or "**JEFFERY WAYNE MCBRIDE JR** " and/or **SUCH OTHER IDENTIFICATION ANY COURT** and/or STATUTORY BODY and/or **GOVERNMENT SERVICE** and/or **AGENTS** and**/or OFFICERS** of such bodies [HEREAFTER "**YOU**"], **HAS ADDRESSED ME AS, I RESPECTFULLY ASK; by WHAT AUTHORITY ARE "YOU" ADDRESSING** me as such?

5. As the **SURETY BOND (BIRTH CERTIFICATE**) has been deposited into the **COURT, WHAT EVIDENCE** does the **COURT** have that I, as **a WO/MAN** who is not lawfully entitled to the **BENEFITS of a BIRTH CERTIFICATE**, have any **SURETY** in this matter?

6. As **GOVERNMENT** is the **SOLE SIGNATORY PARTY** on the **SURETY BOND (BIRTH CERTIFICATE**), with **SOLE AND FULL SURETY** as **TRUSTEE** for the **LEGAL NAME, WHAT EVIDENCE** do **YOU** have that I am **a TRUSTEE** for the **LEGAL NAME. WHAT EVIDENCE** do **YOU** have that I am a **TRUSTEE** and have **ANY SURETY** with respect to **ANY NAME?**

7. **WHAT EVIDENCE** do **YOU** have, that I am an **OFFICER**, an **AGENT**, a **TRUSTEE** and/or an **EMPLOYEE** of the **CROWN? WHAT EVIDENCE** do "**YOU**" have of any **WARRANT OF AGENCY** for the principal?

8. **WHAT EVIDENCE** do "**YOU**" have that there has been any meeting of the minds, any **PROPER NOTICE** given, any considerable **CONSIDERATION** offered, or that I have **ANY INTENT** to **CONTRACT** in this matter?

As such, I am returning your **OFFER, DECLINED**, for immediate **DISCHARGE** and **CLOSURE.**

TRUST NUMBER: 21CP200858
EXHIBIT 3333

The use of such instruments (body attachment, bench warrants, arrests, Including garnishment of wages etc.) presumably is a method to "streamline" arresting people and circumventing the Fourth Amendment to the United States Constitution, and is used as a debt-collecting tool using unlawful arrests and imprisonment to collect a debt or perceived debt. .

"by definition, probable cause to arrest can only exist in relation to criminal conduct; civil disputes cannot give rise to probable cause"; **Paff v. Kaltenbach, 204 F.3d 425, 435 (3rd Cir. 2000)** (Fourth Amendment prohibits law enforcement officers from arresting citizens without probable cause. See, **Illinois v. Gates, 462 U.S. 213 (1983)**, therefore, no body attachment, bench warrant or arrest order may be issued.

If a person is arrested on less than probable cause, the United States Supreme Court has long recognized that the aggrieved party has a cause of action under 42 U.S.C. §1983 for violation of Fourth Amendment rights. **Pierson v. Ray, 386 U.S. 547, 87 S.Ct. 1213 (1967). Harlow v. Fitzgerald, 457 U.S. 800, 818** (there can be no objective reasonableness where officials violate clearly established constitutional rights such as--(a) United States Constitution, Fourth Amendment (including Warrants Clause), Fifth Amendment (Due Process and Equal Protection), Ninth Amendment (Rights to Privacy and Liberty), Fourteenth Amendment (Due Process and Equal Protection).

NOTICE OF DEMAND OF OATH OF OFFICE and STATEMENT OF JURISDICTION

PUBLIC NOTICE FOR:

d/b/a: Judge – **FOR THE Superior Court of GEORGIA For FULTON County**
AND FOR THE COUNTY COURT OF GEORGIA FOR FULTON COUNTY
and Court Clerks, sundry employees, officers, agents, et al.

a/k/a: PUBLIC SERVANTSs – **FULTON** County, **GEORGIA**
and Court Clerks, sundry employees, officers, agents, et al.

Peace Officer D. Ikegwa

d/b/a: Peace Officer D. Ikegwu Unit# 2922 Div. patrol – **FOR THE College Park Police Department of GEORGIA For FULTON County and Municipal Court of The City Of College Park**
AND FOR THE COUNTY COURT OF GEORGIA FOR FULTON COUNTY
and Court Clerks, sundry employees, officers, agents, et al.

a/k/a: PUBLIC SERVANTSs – **FULTON** County, **GEORGIA**
and Court Clerks, sundry employees, officers, agents, et al.

TRUST NUMBER: 21CP200858
EXHIBIT 3333

NOTICE TO PRINCIPAL IS NOTICE TO AGENT
NOTICE TO AGENT IS NOTICE TO PRINCIPAL

Point of Law

All contracts commence with an offer and only become binding upon acceptance. **See Farnsworth on Contracts ©2004 by E. Allan Farnsworth, Third Edition, Aspen Publisher, ISBN: 0-7355-4605-3 (Vol. 1) 3.3**

The People's Contract a/k/a "The Constitution of the United States of America" or "This Constitution" (Articles 1-6; Bill of Rights 1-10) mandates an oath of office for all officers in public service to wit: " . . . the judges in every State shall be bound thereby, any Thing in the Constitution or Laws of an State to the Contrary notwithanding."

Further, the **CONSTITUTION OF THE STATE OF GEORGIA** mandates every PERSON elected or appointed subscribe to an oath that he will "support"[1] and "maintain" the Constitution for the United States and the constitution of "this state," (20.1) and purchase a faithful performance bond as a good faith pledge that the Officer will conduct his/her duties per the requirements of both constitutions "before entering upon his duties" in relation to his/her public office as a **PUBLIC SERVANT (22.19; NMSA 7-2-2 thru 7-2-7).**

BE IT KNOWN to ALL COURT OFFICIALS AND ATTORNEYS et al. that I accept your oath(s) of office d/b/as "Judge" or "other" for the County of **MISSOURI** provided that you are competent to conduct the duties of office having subscribed to the required oath and posted a faithful performance bond as required by fundamental law.

FURTHERMORE NOTICES *all custodians of the public trust* to *release all* custodial holding[s] completely leaving no residue being held by any custodian whatsoever and return all property or interest either tangible, intangible, *ledger*[financial] and real property in this matter as I am the sole surviving heir of my parent's precious and lawful love, and have the only absolute claim of dominion.

Trinsey v Pagliaro, D.C.Pa. 1964, 229 F.Supp. 647.

It's a VIOLATION of the 11th Amendment for a FOREIGN CITIZEN to INVOKE the JUDICIAL POWER of the State.

Article XI.

The Judicial power of the United States shall not be construed to extend to any suit in law or equity, commenced or prosecuted against one of the United States by Citizens of another State, or by Citizens or Subjects of any Foreign State.

US citizens (FEDERAL CITIZENS) are FOREIGN to the several States and SUBJECTS of the FEDERAL UNITED STATES/STATE of NEW COLUMBIA/DISTRICT OF COLUMBIA.

TRUST NUMBER: 21CP200858
EXHIBIT 3333

Attorneys are considered FOREIGN AGENTS under the FOREIGN AGENTS REGISTRATION ACT (FARA) and are SUBJECTS of the BAR ASSOCIATION.

"An attorney for the plaintiff cannot admit evidence into the court. He is either an attorney or a witness".

(Trinsey v. Pagliaro D.C.Pa. 1964, 229 F. Supp. 647)

Should the above statements not be true, then let the record be corrected or it will stand as truth.

All rights Reserved,

[1] **Support**, n. 5. In general, the **maintenance** or sustaining of any thing **without suffering it to fail, decline or languish.** Daniel Webster's Dictionary (1828). [Emphasis added]

Maintain, v.t. [L. manus and teneo.] 1. To hold, preserve or keep in any state or condition; to support; to sustain; not suffer to fail or decline. **Daniel Webster's Dictionary (1828).**

<u>I hereby give you ten (10) days to reply to this notice from the above date with a notice sent using recorded post and signed under full commercial liability and penalties of perjury, assuring and promising me that all of the replies and details given to the above requests are true and without deception, fraud or mischief. Your said failure to provide the aforementioned documentation within ten (10) days, from the above date, to validate the debt, will constitute your agreement to the following terms:</u>

That the debt did not exist in the first place;
OR
It has already been paid in full;
AND
That any damages suffer, you will be held culpable;
That any negative remarks made to a credit reference agency will be removed;
You will no longer pursue this matter any further.
You agree to pay all fee schedules.

Please Note: I wish to deal with this matter in writing and I do not give your organization permission to contact me by telephone. Should you do so, I must warn you that the calls could constitute 'harassment' and I may take action under Section 1 of the Protection from Harassment Act 1997 and the Administration of Justice Act 1970 S.40, which makes it a Criminal Offence for a creditor or a creditor's agent to make demands (for money), which are aimed at causing 'alarm, distress or humiliation', because of their frequency or manner.

STATMENT OF FACTS

TRUST NUMBER: 21CP200858
EXHIBIT 3333

<u>*For the record we wish to effect payment immediately. What is the sum certain on the penal funds?*</u>

*Affiant is a national of the nation/state of Illinois, as contemplated by the act of congress evidenced and restated at **8 U.S.C. 1101(a)(2)**. Affiant is aware and knows that the U.S. bankruptcy is verified in **Senate Report No. 93-519 93rd. Congress, 1st Session (1973), Summary of Emergency Power Statues, "Executive Orders 6073, 6102, 6111, and by Executive Order 6260 on March 9th, 1933 under the "Trading with the Enemy Act (Sixty-Fifth Congress, Session 1, Chapters 105, 106, October 6th, 1917, and as further codified at 12 U.S.C.A. 95(a) and (b)** as amended.*

- I conditionally accept all facts in the claim if the respondent can prove authority to make presentments
- I conditionally accept for value and return for value the presumption I have a duty to show cause for actions upon proof of claim that it is not public policy of the **UNITED STATES** under **HJR-192** <u>to not pay debts at law but instead to exchange consideration upon a dollar for dollar basis to discharge or offset a liability.</u>
- I conditionally accept for value and return for value the presumption I have a duty to show cause for my actions with the bank or respondent upon proof of claim that without money of account (*as established under* **Article One, Sections 10**, *clause one, of the Organic Constitution of the Untied States of America*) in circulation that the only commercial consideration that exists is each and every person's exemption by way of a prepaid account operated by the United States Secretary of Treasury.

Affiant is aware and knows that a certificate of live birth (certificate of title) is a bond that evidences title held by the **Depositary Trust Company (DTCC).** The issuer has legal title; you have equitable title up until you partner up to share equitable title with the United States. SS-5 creates the UPPERCASE NAME which is surety for the Vessel. The Vessel is the body and evidenced on the application by length, weight, and footprints. A body manifested into the sea of commerce. The beneficiary is supposed to be Me, Myself, and I. But the Depositary Trust Company (DTCC) is at 55 Water Street New York City and operates both the public and the private side. Under Civil Rico Racketeering Laws **18 U.S.C.** 1964 as corporations may have established a pattern of racketeering activity by using mail to collect an unlawful debt. If proven there is a conspiracy to deprive of property without due process is various constitutional injuries under **18 U.S.C.A. 241**. *Knowledge and neglect to prevent a United States Constitutional wrong. 31 U.S.C. 5118 (d)2 None can ask for payment in specific coin. 31 U.S.C. 3123* There is no money, so no one can demand payment... the United States will discharge debt dollar for dollar.

Affiant is aware and knows that legal tender (FEDERAL RESERVE NOTES) are not good and lawful money of the United States. See Rains V. State,State, 226 S.W .18

Affiant is aware and knows that the Undersigned affiant has been estopped from using and has no access to ' lawful Constitutional Money of exchange' (see U.S. Constitution- Article 1 Section 10) to "pay debts at law", and pursuant to HJR-192, can only discharge fines, fees, debts, and judgements 'dollar for dollar' via commercial paper or upon Affiant's Exemption.

TRUST NUMBER: 21CP200858
EXHIBIT 3333

There are no judicial courts in America and there has no been since 1789. Judges do no enforce statutes and codes. Executive Administrators enforce statutes and codes. (FRC V. GE 281 US464 KELLER V. PE 261 US 428, 1 STAT. 138-178

I HEREBY notice that I am the executor of the Cestui Que Vie Trust of **JEFFERY WAYNE MCBRIDE JR** according to Title 26 sections 303 & 7701, companies, corporations, and associations and trusts are all decedents. This means my all UPPERCASE NAME IS A LEGAL ESTATE. My ALL UPPERCASE NAME falls into this class. I direct all of the affairs and financial affairs of **JEFFERY WAYNE MCBRIDE JR**

The following documents are needed to move forward in these matters
All tax bond receipts 1099 OID, 1099A, 1099C

The authorization from the **INTERNAL REVENUE SERVICE** to go forward with the above mentioned
account number [26 U.S.C. 2032A(e)11]
Employee Affidavit [Title 5 U.S.C. 3333]
Registration [Title 22 U.S.C. 611 and 612]

Please provide all of the following information and submit the appropriate forms and paperwork back to me along with an affidavit signed in accordance with 28 U.S.C. 1746 for validation and proof of claim.

I affirm that all statement, facts, and information presented in this affidavit/ writ are correct and are presented as evidence for the record. Evidence, exhibit, Information, and facts are placed in Evidence in this case, and As I am reserving and retaining all my rights and affirm to the best of my knowledge and belief.

MAY ALL PARTIES BE MINDFUL OF 48 CFR, 48 U.S.C., UNIFORM COMMERICAL CODES 1-308, 3-402, 3-419 3-501,

Affiant is aware and know that the various and numerous references to case law, legislative history, state and federal statutes/ codes, Federal Reserve Bank Publications, Supreme Court decisions, the Uniform Commercial Codes, U.S. Organic Constitutional, and general recognized maxims of Law as cited herein and throughout establish the following:

A) That the U.S. Federal government and the several United States did totally and completely debase the organic Lawful Constitutional Coin of the several States of the Union of the United States.
B) That the Federal Government and the several United States have and continue to breach the express mandates of Article 1 Section 10 of the Federal Constitution regarding the minting and circulation of lawful coin.
C) That the lawful coin (i.e. organic medium of exchange) and the former ability to PAY DEBTS has been replaced with fiat, paper currency, with the limited capacity to only discharge debts.

TRUST NUMBER: 21CP200858
EXHIBIT 3333

D) *That Congress of the United States did legislate and provide the American People a remedy/ means to discharge all debt "dollar for dollar" via HJR-192 due to the declared Bankruptcy of the Corporate United States via the abolishment of Constitutional Coin and Currency.*
No Assured value, no liability, errors, nor omissions excepted. All rights reserved and retain without recourse-non-assumpsit

FURTHER AFFIANT SAITH NOT.

Subscribed and sworn, without prejudice, and with all rights reserved,
(Printed Name**: :Jeffery Wayne- of The Family: McBride Jr.**
Principal, by Special Appearance, proceeding Sui Juris.

Signed:_____
Date:_____

On this _____ day of _____, _____, before me, the undersigned, a Notary Public in and for _____, personally appeared the above-signed, known to me to be the one whose name is signed on this instrument, and has acknowledged to me that s/he has executed the same.

Signed:_____
Printed Name:_____
Date:_____
Address:_____

TRUTH AFFIDAVIT

IN THE NATURE OF SUPPLEMENTAL

RULES FOR ADMINISTRATIVE AND MARITIME CLAIMS RULES C(6)

Grant of Exclusive power of attorney to conduct all tax, business, and legal affairs of principal person.

POWER OF ATTORNEY IN FACT

JEFFERY WAYNE MCBRIDE JR, or any derivative thereof, **C/O [GENERAL Delivery 1101 E Cumberland Ave Ste 201H-108 Tampa, Florida [33602]** is the Copyright belonging to I, Me, My, Myself addressee **:Jeffery W- of the family: McBride Jr** Non-domestic **c/o General Delivery 1101 E Cumberland Ave Ste 201H-108 [33602]** a Living Soul, a man, Principal, and Title owner with Power of Attorney in Fact. To take exclusive charge of, manage, and conduct all of my tax, business and legal affairs, and for such purpose to act for My Copyright, without limitation on the powers necessary to carry out this exclusive purpose of attorney in fact as authorized:

(A) To take possession of, hold, and manage My Copyrights real estate and all other property;

(B) To receive money or property paid or delivered from any source for My Copyright;

(C) To deposit funds in, make withdrawals from, or sign checks or drafts against any account standing in my name individually or jointly in any bank or other depository, to cash coupons, bonds, or certificates of deposits, to endorse checks, notes or other documents in my Copyright name; to have access to, and place items in or remove them from, any safety deposit box standing in My Copyright, individually or jointly, and otherwise to conduct bank transactions or business for me in my name;

(D) To pay for My Copyright, any just debts and expenses, including reasonable expenses incurred by my attorney in fact **:Jeffery W- of the family: McBride Jr**, in exercising this exclusive power of attorney.

(E) To retain any investments, invest, and to invest in stocks, bonds, or other securities, or in real estate or other property for My Copyright;

(F) To give general and special proxies or exercise rights of conversion or rights with respect to shares or securities, to deposit shares or securities with, or transfer them to protective committees or similar bodies, to join in any reorganization and pay assessments or subscriptions called for in connection with shares or securities;

(G) To sell, exchange, lease, give options, and make contracts concerning real estate or other property for such considerations and on such terms as my attorney in fact **:Jeffery W- of the family: McBride Jr** may consider prudent;

(H) To improve or develop real estate, to construct, alter, or repair building structures and appurtenances or real estate; to settle boundary lines, easements, and other rights with respect to real estate; to plant, cultivate, harvest, and sell or otherwise dispose of crops and timber, and do all things necessary or appropriate to good husbandry.

(I) To provide for the use, maintenance, repair, security, or storage of my tangible property;

(J) To purchase and maintain such policies of insurance against liability, fire, casualty, or other risks as my attorney **:Jeffery W- of the family: McBride Jr** may consider prudent;

The Agent/Living Soul/a Man, **:Jeffery W- of the family: McBride Jr**, is hereby authorized by law to act for and in control of My Copyright **JEFFERY WAYNE MCBRIDE JR**, or any derivative thereof. In addition, through the exclusive power of attorney, to contract for all business and legal affairs of My Copyright **JEFFERY WAYNE MCBRIDE JR**

The term "exclusive" shall be construed to mean that while these powers of attorney are in force, only the attorney in fact may obligate The Copyright in these matters, and The Copyright cannot obligate with regard to the same. This grant of Exclusive Power is Irrevocable during the lifetime of the Title Owner/Living Soul/Man **:Jeffery W- of the family: McBride**

This instrument is lawful and Enforcing **NUNC PRO TUNC and FOREVERMORE.**

Acceptance:

JEFFERY WAYNE MCBRIDE JR , GRANTOR

My Copyright Executed and sealed by the voluntary act of my own hand.

Executed without the UNITED STATES, I declare under penalty of perjury under the laws of the Georgia Republic that the foregoing is true and correct.

I, the above named exclusive attorney in fact, do hereby accept the fiduciary interest of the

herein-named COPYRIGHT and will execute the herein-granted powers-of-attorney with due diligence.

:Jeffery W- of the family: McBride Jr, Title Owner, Attorney in Fact, With the Autograph

_____

Signature of Attorney In Fact All Rights Reserved U.C.C. 1-308

FURTHER AFFIANT SAITH NOT.
Subscribed and sworn, without prejudice, and with all rights reserved,
(Printed Name:) **:JEFFERY W:** of the family name **:MCBRIDE JR**
Principal, by Special Appearance, proceeding Sui Juris.

Signed:_____
Date:_____

On this _____ day of _____, _____, before me, the undersigned, a Notary Public in and for _____, personally appeared the above-signed, known to me to be the one whose name is signed on this instrument, and has acknowledged to me that s/he has executed the same.

Signed:_____
Printed Name:_____
Date:_____

CASE NUMBER: 21CP200858
EXHIBIT 54697

THE HONORABLE COURTS OF GEORGIA
AFFIDAVIT

DEMAND TO DISMISS

Affiant, :Jeffery Wayne – Jr : Of The Family McBride sui juris, a common man of the Republic People, does swear and affirm that Affiant has scribed and read the foregoing facts, and in accordance with the best of Affiant's firsthand knowledge and conviction, such are true, correct, complete, and not misleading, the truth, the whole truth, and nothing but the truth.

JEFFERY WAYNE MCBRIDE JR

VS

STATE OF GEORGIA

DEMAND to DISMISS

:Jeffery Wayne – Jr : Of The Family McBride
Demands to move the court to dismiss this case for the following reasons.

1. THE RESERVATION OF MY RIGHTS.

:Jeffery Wayne – Jr : Of The Family McBride
explicitly reserve all of my rights. UCC 1-308 which was formally UCC 1-207.
§ 1-308. Performance or Acceptance Under Reservation of Rights.
a) A party that with explicit reservation of rights performs or promises performance or assents to performance in a manner demanded or offered by the other party does not thereby prejudice the rights reserved. Such words as "without prejudice," "under protest," or the like are sufficient.

CASE NUMBER: 21CP200858
EXHIBIT 54697

2. FURTHER ADVISEMENT

This is to advise that all of the actions of the court and all others in these cases against JEFFERY WAYNE MCBRIDE JR are in violation of ...

A. USC TITLE 18 > PART I > CHAPTER 13 > § 242 Deprivation of rights under color of law

B. USC TITLE 18 > PART I > CHAPTER 13 > § 241 Conspiracy against rights

WHEREFORE, :Jeffery Wayne – Jr : Of The Family McBride , demands and prays for the foregoing speedy relief.
Kindest and warmest regards,

Signed_____
Without prejudice UCC 1-308
:Jeffery Wayne – Jr : Of The Family McBride .

Notification of reservation of rights
UCC1-308/UCC 1-207

PUBLIC
Your name here, :Jeffery Wayne – Jr : Of The Family McBride , sui juris

THIS IS A PUBLIC COMMUNICATION TO ALL
All rights reserved
UCC1-308
Notice to agents is notice to principles
Notice to principles is Notice to Agents
Applications to all successors and assigns

CASE NUMBER: 21CP200858
EXHIBIT 54697

All are without excuse

Let it be known to all that I, your name here explicitly reserves all of my rights. **UCC1-308 which was formally UCC 1-207.**
Further, let all be advised that all actions commenced against me may be in violation of,...
USC TITLE 18 > PARTI > CHAPTER 13 > § 242 Deprivation of rights under color of law
USC TITLE 18 > PARTI > CHAPTER 13 > § 241 Conspiracy against rights
Wherefore all have undeniable knowledge.

Signed _____ sui juris,
This Affidavit is dated_____.

NOTARY PUBLIC
STATE OF COUNTY OF_____

Subscribed and sworn to before me, a Notary Public, the above signed your name here.

This day of _____, 2021
Notary Public

MY COMMISSION EXPIRES:_____

CASE NUMBER: 21CP200858
EXHIBIT 54697

TRUST NUMBER: 21CP200858
EXHIBIT 911

You are hereby ordered to CEASE AND DESIST any/all actions!

You are hereby in RECEIPT OF NOTICE under the **Fair Debt Collections Practices Act, RCW 62A.3, RCW 19.16 and 19.86** regarding your above referenced file number and presented with a CONDITIONAL ACCEPTANCE OFFER.

If you can state your claim, please provide that information & fill out the enclosed IRS form W9. I will need your EIN number to forward to IRS for collections via form 1099/1096 stating your taxable gain on any payments made or amounts you may incur in the self executing contract section if you pursue this matter without proof of claim.

In an effort to settle this matter in the most efficient possible manner, I hereby CONDITIONALLY ACCEPT your demand for payment in the above named matter upon your complete and total fulfillment of the following conditions:

Condition #1. A Notarized copy of the ORIGINAL WET INK SIGNED CONTRACT PER per **15 U.S.C. 1681** and all other supporting documentation that give rise to and lawfully support the alleged obligations your firm now claims is owed.

Condition #2. Provide me with a sworn and notarized Affidavit, signed under Penalty of Perjury as follows:

    a. That your client is the bona fide party in interest and Holder in Due Course of the aforementioned Contract, and that they can and will further produce said ORIGINAL WET INK SIGNED CONTRACT per **Section 604 of the Fair Credit Reporting Act** AND **15 U.S.C. 1681** in Condition #1 above.

    b. The names, addresses, dates and durations of time during which any and all persons, Corporations, associations, legal firms or any other parties and/or entities who may have had or presently now have any interest in the collection or legal proceedings regarding this alleged obligation.

    c. That as a claimed debt collector, you have not purchased evidence of this alleged debt and are proceeding solely in the name of the original contracting party or parties.

    d. That you know, understand and agree that certain clauses in a contract of adhesion are unenforceable unless the party to whom the contract is extended could have selectively rejected the clause.

    e. That both you and your firm have taken reasonable and prudent due diligence to verify that the amount claimed as owed is, in fact, a legitimate and bona fide debt, prior to instigating this action and making said claim, and that all relevant correspondence, challenges, denials and counter claims by me have been fully and thoroughly reviewed by and adequately answered by your firm both prior to and since initiating this claim.

    f. That since initiating this claim, your firm, or associates under your employ, did not contact me at my residence more than three times in any given week or at any other unreasonable time or in any unreasonable manner.

    g. That you, your firm or associates under your employ, did not fail to identify themselves as a debt collector in any manner or at any time pertaining to this alleged claim.

Condition #3. Provide written verification in the form of a signed, sworn and Notarized Affidavit from the stated creditor that you are authorized to act on their behalf in this alleged debt collection action.

Condition #4. Provide the total account and general ledger statement showing the full and complete Accounting of the alleged obligation you are attempting to collect from me, signed and sworn to by the authorized person responsible for maintaining these records and having first-hand knowledge as to their accuracy and authenticity, and are able and willing to testify to same under oath to that effect.

Condition #5. Provide Certified and Notarized copies of documents showing that you are or represent a bona fide creditor in a collection process to include:

    a. A notarized copy of certified documents evidencing that you are allowed to conduct business in the State of Oregon as a collection agency.

    b. A notarized copy of the Bond on file with the State of Washington allowing your firm to operate as a collection agency.

c. A notarized copy of the assignment letter including production of the signatures and status showing your firm as holders in due course of the alleged claim.

Condition #6. Provide the statutes and enforcing regulations, both Federal and State, which clearly and unequivocally make me liable for this alleged debt.

Condition #7. Provide the statutes and enforcing regulations, both Federal and State, which clearly and unequivocally allow for the collection of this alleged debt.

Condition #8. Provide proof that your "Notice of Debt Collection", is authorized by such Statutes and enforcing Regulations.

Condition #9. Provide proof of all relevant signatures and your status as Holders in Due Course of this alleged claim.

Condition #10. Provide the name(s), address(es) and telephone number(s) of the bona fide creditor(s) pertaining to this alleged debt.

Condition #11. If you are acting as an Agent, provide certified copies of the registered claim upon which you are collecting, showing the name(s) of any and all debtors and the respective bona fide creditor(s) as the secured party(s).

Condition #12. Provide the national and regional credit and debit card network Rules and Regulations governing electronic payments and ATM transactions; specifically the production of all versions of the manual in each case for each service/ buyer/ successor/ transferee regarding this alleged claim.

Condition #13. Provide a sworn and Notarized Affidavit, signed under Penalty of Perjury, that all the Rules and Regulations of the National and Regional credit and debit card network Rules and Regulations were never, at any time, violated or circumvented to the detriment of the Affiant pertaining to this alleged claim.

Condition #14. Provide verifiable proof that any actual "money" was ever created or loaned to me by the named creditor(s) whom you claim to represent, and not mere bookkeeping entries that were made by them in an attempt to establish the alleged obligation or debt, and in which case, this entire matter would constitute fraud on their part, as well as now yours.

NOTICE:

Contacting me again without first properly documenting that I have any obligation to you or

TRUST NUMBER: 21CP200858
EXHIBIT 911

your claimant pertaining to the above referenced trust numbers, after <u>Verifiable Receipt of this Notice of Conditional Acceptance,</u> will establish and constitute that you deliberately intend to use interstate communications in a scheme of fraud by using further threats, intimidations, deceptions and/or enticements to coerce me to commit some act creating a legal obligation and/or disability where none exists, previously or presently, as well as constituting that you and/or your firm knew or should have known that by such communication, what you have heretofore attempted to do was, and is, false and therefore unlawful. Moreover, until or unless you have fully satisfied all of my demands and claims as stated herein and previously, as well as provided by numerous laws and regulations, both Federal and State, pertaining to this alleged claim, which the courts and/or others who rely upon such written communication may well judge such acts by you as deliberately intended to impair or damage my credit rating, my reputation, my standing in the community as well as to intentionally inflict financial and emotional harm upon me, and assure you that you do so at your own peril and risk.

You have twenty one (10) days from receipt of this Conditional Acceptance to respond on a point-by- point basis, via sworn Affidavit, under your full commercial liability, signing under penalty of perjury, that the facts contained therein are true, correct and complete, and not misleading in any manner whatsoever. **Declarations are an insufficient response,** as declarations permit lying by omissions, which no honorable draft may contain.

Your failure to accept my Conditional Offer of Settlement by producing each and every requested answer, record and/or documentation, or in the alternative, sending me written withdrawal of your claim, (summary judgment), will constitute your stipulation that I have no duty or obligation to any portion of the above aforementioned debt whatsoever, and that you have no right or basis to pursue any further collection.

Be advised that notice to any agent of the STATE or under courts regarding this Conditional Offer of Acceptance in considered notice to any and all principals. Further, your failure to fully and completely respond on a point-by-point basis, as well as ANY ACTIVITY by you or your firm to secure payment with a "Writ of Garnishment", before responding to this <u>Conditional Acceptance,</u> shall be deemed as an Agreement with the facts as stated in the attached Affidavit,

TRUST NUMBER: 21CP200858
EXHIBIT 911

and shall be further deemed an <u>Automatic Dishonor of this Conditional Acceptance</u> and agreement to the COURTS to the immediate payment of $75,000.00 USD, payable to

Jeffery Wayne McBride Jr as compensating damages.

Signed from "without" the "United States" in accordance with 28 U.S.C., Sec. 1746(1). All rights are reserved without prejudice, UCC 1-207 and RCW 62A.1-207.

I have disputed this unlawful debt ; therefore, until validated you know your information concerning this debt is inaccurate. Thus, if you have already reported this debt to any credit-reporting agency (CRA) or Credit Bureau (CB) and any other GOVERMENTAL AGENCIES then, you must immediately inform them of my dispute with this debt. Reporting information that you know to be inaccurate or failing to report information
correctly violates the Fair Credit Reporting Act § 1681s-2. Should you pursue a judgment without validating this debt, I will inform the SECRETARY OF STATE AND ATTORNEY GENERAL and request the case be dismissed based on your failure to comply with the FDCPA and for reservation of rights.

x_____

Jeffery Wayne McBride Jr

Authorized Representative
A Living man

_____2021
Date

TRUST NUMBER: 21CP200858
EXHIBIT 911

RE: JEFFERY W MCBRIDE JR
GENERAL DELIVERY 1101 E CUMBERLAND AVE STE 201H-108 TAMPA, FL 33602

Declaration by Affidavit in Support of Conditional Acceptance

Having been duly sworn, Affiant declares the following:

1. Jeffery W McBride Jr, a living man Affiant, is competent to state the matter included in this Declaration, has knowledge of the facts and hereby declares that to the best of her knowledge, that the statements made in this Affidavit are true, correct, complete and not meant to mislead and are made under full commercial liability.

2. Affiant is not in possession of documentation that proves Respondent's claim that they have the authority to enforce a collection against Affiant.

3. Affiant is not in possession of documentation that proves Respondent's claim that there is a bona fide creditor with respect to Affiant.

4. Affiant is not in possession of documentation that proves Respondent's claim that they represent a bona fide creditor with respect to Affiant.

5. Affiant is not in possession of documentation that proves Respondent's claim that they have a registered commercial claim against Affiant.

6. Affiant is not in possession of documentation that proves Respondent's claim that Affiant is a party to a security agreement supporting their claim.

7. Affiant is not in possession of documentation that proves Respondent's alleged obligation that is now claimed as owed.

8. Affiant is not in possession of any documentation, statute or enforcing regulations that proves Respondent's claim that Affiant is clearly and unequivocally liable for this alleged debt.

9. Affiant is not in possession of any documentation that provides the statutes and enforcing regulations which clearly and unequivocally allows for the collection of this debt as Respondent asserts in their "Writ of Garnishment".

10. Affiant is not in possession of any documentation that proves Respondent's "Notice of Debt Collection" is authorized by statute and enforcing regulation.

11. Affiant is not in possession of any documentation that proves Respondent's proof of signatures and status as holders in due course.

12. Affiant is not in possession of documents that provide and prove the names, addresses, and telephone numbers of the bona fide creditors asserted by Respondent.

TRUST NUMBER: 21CP200858
EXHIBIT 911

13. Affiant is not in possession of documents that provide and prove whether Respondent is or is not acting in the capacity of an agent.

14. Affiant is not in possession of any documents that prove the creditor asserted by Respondent is in fact the secured party and/or holder in due course.

15. Affiant is not in possession of any documents that prove or disprove the creditor asserted by Respondent has complied at all times with national and regional credit and debit card network rules and regulations governing electronic payments and ATM transactions.

16. Affiant is not in possession of any documents that prove that the creditor asserted by Respondent ever did loan Affiant any real money.

Further Affiant sayeth not.

X_____ _____2021
Jeffery Wayne McBride Jr
Authorized Representative
A Living man

This is a private communication and is intended to affect an out-of-court settlement of this matter. Conduct yourself accordingly. Should any provision on this agreement be found to not be enforceable by order of a court of competent jurisdiction, it shall not adversely affect any other provision of this agreement and reasonable opportunity and effort shall be taken to modify it to become enforceable.

NOTICE TO THE PRINCIPAL IS NOTICE TO THE AGENT

NOTICE TO THE AGENT IS NOTICE TO THE PRINCIPAL

Applicable to all successors and assigns

Silence is Acquiescence/Agreement/Dishonor

Executed on this _____ by: _____

:Jeffery -W of the family :McBride, Authorized Representative for JEFFERY WAYNE MCBRIDE JR

CC   **Federal Trade Commission**
    Consumer Complaint
    600 Pennsylvania Avenue, NW
    Washington, DC 20580

TRUST NUMBER: 21CP200858
EXHIBIT 911

CC   GEORGIA DEPARTMENT OF JUSTICE
Chris Carr Attorney General
c/o 40 Capitol Square, SW
Atlanta, GA 30334

AFFIDAVIT of TRUTH

Sworn under penalties of perjury

Signature(s) of Real Party in Interest:

Printed Name: :Jeffery W- of the family :McBride

Signature: _____

EIN/SSN: 82-7076969

Failure to produce a contract in accordance with the above guidelines may illustrate that the alleged debt claimed owed was misrepresented and sold to third party debt collectors fraudulently. I am requesting a full removal of Derogatory reporting in my Credit File from all three Credit Reporting Agencies. Failure to notify me at the above address of the completion of these removals within 10 days of receipt of this letter indicates a disregard for the law to exhaust all efforts to resolve this without litigation.

By: :Jeffery W- McBride_____   By:_____

(Print Name of Authorized Representative)   (Sign Name of Authorized Representative)

NOTARY ACKNOWLEGEMENT

State of _____

County of _____

SUBSCRIBED AND SWORN TO before me by _____, known

to me or proven to me to be the real man signing this document this _____ day of

_____, 2021

WITNESS my hand and official seal.

_____

Notary Public

PUBLIC NOTICE
AFFIDAVIT OF FACT

Peter Joseph: House of Polinski; self aware living man

c/o 420 Jeanette Drive

Utica, NY Near; [13502]

STATE OF NEW YORK   )
) SS   ACKNOWLEDGEMENT
ONEIDA COUNTY   )

AFFIDAVIT OF FACT OF MY PEACEFUL INHABITANCE AS A FREEMAN ON THE LAND

OFFICIAL PUBLIC NOTICE TO THE U.S GOVERNMENT, ALL GOVERNMENTAL AGENTS, STATE, NATIONAL and WORLDWIDE MEDIA AND NEWS STATIONS, THE STATE OF NEW YORK AND ANY AND ALL POLITICAL SUBDIVISIONS THEREOF OF THE U.S GOVERNMENT FOREIGN AND OR DOMESTIC

NOTICE TO AGENT IS NOTICE TO PRINCIPAL NOTICE TO PRINCIPAL IS NOTICE TO AGENT

I **Peter Joseph-House of Polinski**; as a Secured Party, independent, conscience, **free born** and self aware living **Freeman** on the land created under **Almighty God**, on and for the Official Public Record declare and make the **Ultimate** and **Un Rebuttable Declaration** that I **Peter Joseph-House of Polinski**; am a **Peaceful, Non Violent, Friendly, at ease, Unaggressive, Relaxed** and a **Peaceful Inhabitant** on the land know by or rendered as North America. It is never my intention to harm, be a threat, or in any way be a Terrorist to or against the COMMUNITY, U.S., U.S GOVERNMENT, UNITED STATES GOVERNMENT, GOVERNMENTAL AGENCIES, THE STATE OF NEW YROK, PUBLIC OFFICIALS, POLICE OFFICERS, JUDGES, U.S CITIZENS and any and all **AGENCIES** or POLITICAL SUBDIVISIONS

Page 1 of 4   Initials: _____ All Rights Reserved Without
Recourse

PUBLIC NOTICE
AFFIDAVIT OF FACT

THEREOF **FOREIGN** and or **DOMESTIC**. I believe there is no evidence to the contrary and that none exist.

I **Peter Joseph-House of Polinski**; as a Secured Party, independent, conscience, **free born** and self aware living **Freeman** on the land created under **Almighty God**, on and for the Official Public Record declare and make the **Ultimate** and **Un Rebuttable Declaration** that I **Peter Joseph-House of Polinski**; do not nor have I ever had intentions of trying to over throw, War with or harm the **U.S, U.S. GOVERNMENT, UNITED STATES GOVERNMENT, THE STATE OF NEW YORK, U.S CITIZENS** and any and all **POLITICAL AGENCIES** or **SUBDIVISIONS** THEREOF **FOREIGN** and or **DOMESTIC**. I believe there is no evidence to the contrary and that none exist.

I **Peter Joseph-House of Polinski** as a Secured Party, independent, conscience, **free born** and self aware living **Freeman** on the land created under **Almighty God**, on and for the Official Public Record declare and make the **Ultimate** and **Un Rebuttable Declaration** that I **Peter Joseph-House of Polinski**; am a independent, conscience, **free born** common law abiding, taxpaying **American National**, as I pay Gas Tax, Sales Tax, Food Tax etc. Any claims to the contrary that I don't pay Taxes and don't want to pay Taxes must be done in writing by way of Sworn Affidavit on and for the Official Public Record and under penalties of the law including perjury. Anyone making false claims, presumption and or speculations not in writing by way of Sworn Affidavit on and for the Official Public Record and under penalties of the law including perjury will be sued in their unlimited Official and Personal capacity. I believe there is no evidence to the contrary and that none exist.

I **Peter Joseph-House of Polinski**; as a Secured Party, independent, conscience, **free born** and self aware living **Freeman** on the land created under **Almighty God**, on and for the Official Public Record declare and make the Ultimate and **Un Rebuttable Declaration** that I **Peter Joseph-House of Polinski**; have not nor have I ever said, declared or established that I don't have to abide by the law, but what I do state and declare on and for the Official Public Record is that any statue, code or law that is in violation and or conflict with the **organic national Constitution of the Republic of the United States of America Un-Incorporated** is in fact null and void from the beginning. Furthermore any law, code and or statue that is in conflict and is inconsistent with the very purpose and true meaning of the **organic national Constitution of the Republic of the United States of America Un-Incorporated** is in fact null and void, dead, making war with the constitution as well as committing Treason against the American People. For the benefit of all Public Officials, **U.S, U.S. GOVERNMENT, UNITED STATES GOVERNMENT, THE STATE OF NEW YORK, U.S CITIZENS, ALL LOCAL, NATIONAL** and **WORLDWIDE MEDIA AND NEW STATIONS** and any and all **AGENCIES** or **POLITICAL SUBDIVISIONS** THEREOF **FOREIGN** and or **DOMESTIC** it would be in your best interest before making any false claims to first know and understand the organic **national Constitution of the Republic of the United States of America Un-Incorporated** before you can truly say what

Page 2 of 4   Initials: _____ **All Rights Reserved Without Recourse**

PUBLIC NOTICE
AFFIDAVIT OF FACT

the laws are. I **Peter Joseph-House of Polinski**; as a Secured Party, independent, conscience, **free born** and self aware living **Freeman** on the land created under **Almighty God**, on and for the Official Public Record hereby, hereinafter and forever **DEMAND** that anyone involved with the **U.S, U.S. GOVERNMENT, UNITED STATES GOVERNMENT, THE STATE OF NEW YORK, U.S CITIZENS, ALL LOCAL, NATIONAL and WORLDWIDE MEDIA AND NEW STATIONS** and any and all **AGENCIES** or **POLITICAL SUBDIVISIONS** THEREOF **FOREIGN** and or **DOMESTIC** intends to make any Claim to the contrary that it must be done in writing by way of Sworn Affidavit on and for the Official Public Record and under penalties of the law including perjury. Anyone and for the Official Public Record I mean **absolutely** anyone making a **False Claim** against I **Peter Joseph-House of Polinski**; as a Secured Party, independent, conscience, **free born** and self aware living **Freeman** on the land created under **Almighty God**, not in writing by way of Sworn Affidavit on and for the Official Public Record and under penalties of the law including perjury will be sued in their Official as well as Private capacity. I believe there is no evidence to the contrary and that none exist.

NOTICE TO AGENT IS NOTICE TO PRINCILAL NOTICE TO PRINCIPAL IS NOTICE TO AGENT

The Foregoing Instrument is being executed under the hand and seal of the self aware living man and is my **Free-Will act and Deed** so help me **God**.

Autographed under penalties of Perjury.

X_____ UCC 1-308, 3-415;

Peter Joseph-House of Polinski; self aware living man created under **God** ALL RIGHTS RESERVED

STATE OF NEW YORK   )
) SS   ACKNOWLEDGEMENT
COUNTY OF ONEIDA   )

On this _____ day of _____ **2017**, before me the Notary below appeared before me **Peter Joseph-House of Polinski**; to me known to be the **living man** described in and who executed the foregoing instrument and acknowledged before me that he executed the same as his **freewill act and deed.**

Subscribed and affirmed before me, _____, Notary on the _____ Day of _____ 2017. NOTARY PRINT NAME: _____ Date: _____

Page 3 of 4   Initials: _____ All Rights Reserved Without Recourse

PUBLIC NOTICE
AFFIDAVIT OF FACT

NOTARY SIGNATURE: _____ Date: _____

NOTARY SEAL

Commission Expires: _____

Initials: _____ All Rights Reserved Without Recourse

Notice of Intent- Fee Schedule

To Whom It May Concern:

The annexed <u>Notice of Intent – Fee Schedule</u> is a schedule of mandatory fees instated by the Secured Party Creditor, PETER JOSEPH : THE HOUSE OF POLINSKI™, Authorized Signatory Attorney-in-fact on behalf of PETER JOSEPH POLINSKI, Ens Legis. I, PETER JOSEPH : THE HOUSE OF POLINSKI ™, do hereby set forth fees to be instated in any business dealing with PETER JOSEPH POLINSKI™ for any business conducted relevant to this schedule. Fees are due and MUST be paid before said business can commence. In the event that invoicing becomes necessary, invoiced amounts are due fifteen days after day of receipt. If said fees are not met, it is the right of the Secured Party Creditor, PETER JOSEPH : THE HOUSE OF POLINSKI ™, to refuse or void any form of business interaction and/or transaction. Fees are subject to change at any time without prior notice. Secured Party Creditor, PETER JOSEPH : THE HOUSE OF POLINSKI ™, is the only authorized personnel to alter, void, and/or enforce said fees and may do so at any time.

Without Prejudice,

By: _____

Peter Joseph : the House of Polinski
American National
UCC1-308 without prejudice, without recourse
In accordance with Title 8 U.S.C § 1101(a)(21). The
Grantor/Executor/Director/Heir/
Sole Shareholder/Chief Executive Officer
for PETER JOSEPH POLINSKI ESTATE

Acknowledgement

STATE OF WASHINGTON	)
COUNTY OF _____	) Scilicet </br>)

SUBSCRIBED and SWORN (or affirmed) to before me on this _____ day of _____, 2018. a Notary, that PETER JOSEPH POLINSKI, personally appeared and known to me to be the man whose name subscribed to the within instrument and acknowledged to be the same.

Signature of Notary Public: _____

My Commission expires: _____

Notice of Intent- Fee Schedule

Private Easements Schedule
　Penalty for Private Use　　　　　　　　　　　　　　$250000.00

Public Easements Schedule
　Penalty for Public Use　　　　　　　　　　　　　　　$250000.00

These fees will be mandated upon the informant listed on the traffic citation ticket(s), arrest warrants, detention orders, seizure orders.

Produce trade name materials:

a. Name	$ 50000.00
b. Drivers License Number	$ 50000.00
c. Social Security Number	$ 100000.00
d. Retinal Scans	$ 5000000.00
e. Fingerprinting	$ 200000.00
f. Photographing	$ 200000.00
g. DNA	$ 5000000.00
1. Mouth swab	$ 5000000.00
2. Blood samples	$ 5000000.00
3. Urine samples	$ 5000000.00
4. Breathalyzer testing	$ 5000000.00
5. Hair samples	$ 5000000.00
6. Skin samples	$ 5000000.00
7. Clothing samples	$ 5000000.00
8. Forced giving of fluids/samples	$ 5000000.00

Issue Traffic citations and tickets of any traffic nature:

a. Citations	$ 60000.00
b. Warning issued on Paper Ticket	$ 25000.00

Appearance in court because of traffic citations:

a. Time in court min.	$ 75000.00/hr with 1 hour
b. If Fine is imposed	$ 500000.00

Car / Personal Property Trespass, Carjacking, Theft, Interference with Commerce,

a. Agency by Estoppel	$ 50000.00
b. Color of Law	$ 150000.00
c. Implied Color of Law	$ 150000.00
d. Criminal Coercion	$ 500000.00
e. criminal Contempt of court	$ 500000.00

Notice of Intent- Fee Schedule

f.	Estoppel by Election	$	350000.00
g.	Estoppel by Laches	$	350000.00
h.	Equitable Estoppel	$	500000.00
i.	Fraud	$	1000000.00
j.	Fraud upon the court	$	2000000.00
k.	Larceny	$	250000.00
l.	Grand Larceny	$	250000.00
m.	Larceny by Extortion	$	1000000.00
n.	Larceny by Trick	$	1000000.00
o.	Obstruction of Justice	$	100000.00
p.	Obtaining Property by False Pretenses	$	1000000.00
q.	Simulating Legal Process	$	1000000.00
r.	Vexatious Litigation	$	5000000.00
s.	Trespass upon Motor Conveyance	$	100000.00
t.	Unauthorized Relocation of Motor Conveyance	$	100000.00
u.	Seizure of Motor Conveyance	$	100000.00
v.	Theft of License Plate	$	10000.00
w.	Unlawful Lien on Motor Conveyance	$	50000.00

Use of trade name protected material under threat, duress, and/ or coercion:

a.	Name written by the informant	$	250000.00
b.	Drivers License written by informant	$	150000.00
c.	Social Security Number written by informant	$	150000.00
d.	Miscellaneous Material written by informant	$	500000.00

Produce any personal information/property for any kind of business interaction:

a.	Financial Information	$	100000.00
b.	Property inside of motor vehicle	$	150000.00

Time Usage for traffic stops:

PJP-FS-1987

Notice of Intent- Fee Schedule

a. 30 minutes $ 5000.00/30 minutes minimum
b. 60 minutes $ 10000.00
c. 90 minutes $ 15000.00

Court Appearance Schedule

These fees MUST be paid immediately after my case is finished. Failure to pay fines and fees will have an additional fee of $5000.00 for breach of contract.

Demand for Appearance in court:

a. My Appearance
   a. under protest and duress: $ 75000.00/hour
   b. Voluntarily $ 10000.00/hour

Use of trade name material

a. Name
   a. under protest and duress: $ 25000.00
   b. Voluntarily $ 10000.00
b. Drivers License
   a. under protest and duress: $ 25000.00
   b. Voluntarily $ 10000.00
c. Social Security Number
   a. under protest and duress: $ 25000.00
   b. Voluntarily $ 10000.00
d. Miscellaneous Material $ 25000.00
e. Produce any personal information for any kind of business interaction:
   a. Financial Information $ 10000.00
   b. Drivers License $ 10000.00
   c. Social Security Number $ 250000.00
   d. Any documents produced by me $ 10000.00 per document

Time usage for court appearances:

a. 30 minutes

Notice of Intent- Fee Schedule

    a.   Under Protest and Duress $ 33500.00

    b.   Voluntarily $ 10000.00

b. 60 minutes

    a.   Under Protest and Duress $ 75000.00

    b..   Voluntarily $ 20000.00

c. 90 minutes or more

    a.   Under Protest and Duress $ 100500.00

    b.   Voluntarily $ 30000.00

Transgressions-Fee Schedule

Transgressions by public official(s), police officer(s), judge(s), attorney(s), and all other who desire to contract:

a. Failure to honor God Given Rights $20000.00

b. Failure to honor Oath of Office $50000.00

c. Failure to honor Constitutional Oath $50000.00

d. Failure to honor Written and/or Oral Word $ 5000.00

e. Silence/Dishonor/Default $ 5000.00

f. Failure to honor /No Bond $ 5000.00

g. Phone call to telephone number used by Secured Party including from alleged debt collectors $ 5000.00 each

h. Telephone message left on Secured Party phone Service or equipment $ 5000.00 each

i. Use of Street Address/Mailing location of Secured Party $ 5000.00 each

j. Time Waiting for Scheduled Service per hour $ 1000.00 Minimum or

k. Detention from Free Movement and/or cuffed per hour $ 75000.00 Minimum or

Notice of Intent- Fee Schedule

l.	Incarceration per hour	$ 75000.00 Minimum or
m.	Failure to Follow Federal and/or State Statutes, Codes, Rules and/or Regulations	$ 50000.00
n.	Failure to State a Claim upon which Relief Can Be Granted	$250000.00
o.	Failure to Present a Living Injured Party	$100000.00
p.	Failure to Provide Contract Signed by the Parties	$100000.00*
q.	Failure to Provide IRS 1099OID(s), and Other IRS Reporting Form(s) Requirements upon Request	$100000.00*
r.	Default By Non Response or Incomplete Response	$100000.00*
s.	Fraud	$1000000.00*
t.	Racketeering	$1000000.00*
u.	Theft of Public Funds	$1000000.00*
v.	Dishonor in Commerce	$1000000.00*
w.	Failure to pay Counterclaim in full within (30) Thirty Calendar Days of Default as set forth herein	$1000000.00**
x.	Perverting of Justice Judgment	$ 1000000.00*
y.	Use of Common-law Trade-name/Trade-mark After One Warning (per each occurrence)	$ 50000.00 Each
w.	Forcing psychiatric evaluations	$ 500000.00 per day
x.	Refusal to provide adequate and proper nutrition while incarcerated	$ 50000.00 per day
y.	Refusal to provide proper exercise while incarcerated	$ 50000.00 per day
z.	Refusal to provide proper dental care while	

Notice of Intent- Fee Schedule

	Incarcerated	$ 50000.00 per day
aa.	Forced giving of body fluids	$ 5000000.00 per day
bb.	Forced injections/inoculations, vaccines	$ 5000000.00 per day
cc.	Forced separation from marriage contract	$ 160000.00 per day
dd.	Confiscation/kidnapping of a body not a US Citizen	$ 1600000.00 per day
ee.	Corporate State continuing a mortgage for more Than five years in violation of Banking Act of 1864 which takes precedence over current Statutes at large	$ 1600000.00 per day
	Attempted extortion of funds from birth certificate account, Social security account or any other associated accounts by fraud, deception and or Forgery by any agent, entity or corporation charge	$ 6000000.00 per count or
ff.	Attempted extortion of signature	$ 6000000.00 per count or charge
gg.	Attempted forgery of signature	$ 6000000.00 per count or charge

*Per Occurrence and Includes any Third Party Defendant

** All claims are stated in US Dollars which means that a US Dollar will be defined, for this purpose as a One Ounce Silver Coin of .999 pure silver or the equivalent par value as established by law or the exchange rate, as set by the US Mint, whichever is the higher amount, for a certified One Ounce Silver Coin (US Silver Dollar) at the time of the first day of default as set forth herein; if the claim is to be paid in Federal Reserve Notes, Federal Reserve Notes will only be assessed at Par Value as indicated above.

Total damages will be assessed as the total amount of the damages as set forth herein times three (3) for a total of all damages as set forth in subsections a-w added to three (3) times the damages for punitive or other additional damages.

Notice of Intent- Fee Schedule

Kidnapping (If an alleged officer removes free soul more than 5 feet from free soul's property without just cause, it IS kidnapping) $ 5000000.00

Services to others and/or Corporation(s):

    a. Studying $ 500.00 per hour
        while under threat, duress, coercion $ 75000.00 per hour

    b. Analyzing $ 500.00 per hour
        while under threat, duress, coercion $ 75000.00 per hour

    c. Research $ 500.00 per hour
        while under threat, duress, coercion $ 75000.00 per hour

    d. Preparing Documents $ 500.00 per hour
        while under threat, duress, coercion $ 75000.00 per hour

    e. Answering Questions $ 500.00 per hour
        while under threat, duress, coercion $ 75000.00 per hour

    f. Providing Information $ 500.00 per hour
        while under threat, duress, coercion $ 75000.00 per hour

You can make another heading in **Blue** to add metes and bounds or legal descriptions for a foreclosure case. Another example is crops. Loss of each plant, etc. Soil contamination.

Make it your own. Remove this red lettering if it does not apply to you.

If invoiced, payment is due 15 days after receipt date.

Make all payments to:

PETER JOSEPH POLINSKI™
SUITE 614
MARCY, NEW YORK [13403]

™ **Jeffery: Wayne- of the family: McBride** ©, Secured Party and Creditor
Jeffery Wayne McBride Jr,
c/o 1101 E Cumberland Ave Ste 201H-108
Tampa, Florida [33602]
 Republic United States
zip code exempt (DMM 122.32)
Continental America

ATTN: ALL CORPORATE AGENCIES

Date: _____(month), ___(day), 2021

Debtor: ™**JEFFERY WAYNE MCBRIDE JR**©, A LEGAL ENTITY FOR USE IN COMMERCE # **82-7076969**

Creditor: ™ **Jeffery: Wayne- of the family: McBride** ©, A Living, Natural male, and Secured Party.

AFFIDAVIT OF STATUS AS SECURED PARTY AND CREDITOR

I, **Jeffery: Wayne- of the family: McBride** ©, sole authorized agent for the Debtor and by sovereign administrative judgement hereby serve your office with official notice of my lawful standing as Sovereign Secured Party and Creditor. I have supreme authoritative power of attorney, sole security interest, and am the holder in due course of first right of claim over the Debtor, evidenced by a $100,000,000.000.00 commercial lien. I control all affairs of the Debtor, own all assets of the Debtor, and am exempt from levy and relieved of all liability from the Debtor.

NOTICE: The following lawful establishments shall apply upon this notice:

1. All commercial contracts listing the Debtor have been lawfully cancelled, rescinded and revoked and are invalid and unenforceable.
2. As a Sovereign Creditor and Secured Party, I am distinguished and set apart as a separate entity from the Debtor established so by lawful filings into the public and noticed with THE SECRETARY OF STATE, and the UNITED STATES TREASURER. My identity, ™ **JEFFERY WAYNE MCBRIDE JR** ©, is copy written and no agency or person has authorization to use, disclose, report, list or store my name or my personal information for any purpose. Your agency is hereby ordered by Estoppel to remove all computer entries, records, histories, paper documents, references and details in the name of the Debtor and give notice to The Secured Party addressed

below. Failure to comply is considered an International Criminal Action under UNIFORM COMMERCIAL CODES with severe penalty at law.

3. No agency or corporate entity shall have jurisdiction over the Secured Party whatsoever. The flesh and blood man, ™ **Jeffery: Wayne- of the family: McBride** ©, does not require licenses or permission to exercise any natural right.

If you find this AFFIDAVIT OF STATUS AS SECURED PARTY AND CREDITOR to be in error, send rebuttal of the points herein to the Secured Party and Creditor, signed by an authorized representative or attorney for your corporation under oath and agreement to testify to the facts and understanding before a jury under penalty of perjury.

Furthermore: If your corporate agency has any lawful commercial claim against the Sentient, Flesh and Blood, Non-Corporate, Natural Man, **Jeffery: Wayne- of the family: McBride** ©, submit it within (**10) Ten days** of the date of this notice to the address below with valid proof of claim.

If an authorized representative of your agency fails to respond with a valid affidavit of truth in the form of a rebuttal or does not or cannot provide a True Bill of Commerce and a Complete Assessment of any commercial claim against my natural being, or you ignore this notice and remain silent without stating your claim for a period of (**10) Ten days**, **THEN YOU ACCEPT MY CLAIM OF LAWFUL ESTABLISHMENTS HEREIN** by *tacit* agreement and **MY AFFIDAVIT STANDS AS TRUTH IN COMMERCE.** Your default under the maxims of law will constitute your AGREEMENT that any alleged claims against this Living, Breathing, Flesh-and-Blood, Sentient, Natural Man, and Sovereign Creditor and Secured Party, **Jeffery: Wayne- of the family: McBride**© are unfounded in common law and thus **DO NOT AND CANNOT EXIST**.

Honorably,
™ **Jeffery: Wayne- of the family: McBride** ©, Secured Party and Creditor

Jeffery Wayne McBride Jr,
c/o 1101 E Cumberland Ave Ste 201H-108
Tampa, Florida [33602]
     Republic United States
zip code exempt (DMM 122.32)

Authorized Signature: DEBTOR_____

Autograph & Seal By: Secured Party Creditor_____
WITHOUT PREJUDICE-WITHOUT RECOURSE-NON-ASSUMPSIT
All Rights Reserved-Errors & Omissions Excepted

Dated: ____Day of _____, 2021

Notary Public's Signature: _____

Notary Public's Seal

Express Mailing # EF 074130475 US

American Civil "UCC" Arrest WARRANT
For all of the PATRICK DEVINE - Foreign UCC Contract Trust:
by the **American Federal Government "Non-UCC" Owner** standing over the **National Corporate Government** and **Statutory Laws** and **INVOKING** the **1868 Expatriation Act**.

      This **Civil Arrest Warrant** of the below listed **3 Main Foreign UCC Contract Trust** is based upon the **Foreign Commercial Contract GSA Form SF30**, as **Ordered Contract Cancellations** and the **American Peoples' Powers** and **Rights** as the **true American Owners**, as it is addressed in the **Federal Government - _American Commandment_ Laws** known as the **People** and **State Sovereignty Amendments # 9 & 10**; which are (*Non-Commercial and Non-Corporate*) and to be **enforced** by the *Subservient* **National Corporate Governments**, as they are laid out in the National Constitutions and the Statutes at Large, this includes the State Republic Governments.

      The below addressed **3 Main Foreign** and **Deceptive UCC Contract Trust** are operated as **Commercial Non-Construction Contracts** but they are still operating under the same type of Contract Bondage requirements by having **3 Key Parties** and **2 Bonds**. The 3 Key Parties are the **Owner** (*originally* per the **BANKRUPTCY OF THE FOREIGN CONTRACTORS** was to be the _Principal Assured Obligee_ but by **CONTRACTOR's hidden contract deception** was made out to be the _Principal Obligor_), the **CONTRACTOR** (as the **Trustee** and an **Unaccountable Beneficiary**) and the **Surety** (*which was to be the fictional person and the _sole Obligor_ on the Bonds*) and the **2 Contract Bonds** are the **Performance Bond (SF-1418)** and **Payment Bond (SF-1416)**.

      Therefore per my **Owner's Right** and **my Authority as the Cancelling party**, I am using the attached **SF-30 forms** and this **Civil Arrest Warrant** to **Cancel** and **End** the below listed **UCC Contract Trust** by destroying their force, validity, or effectiveness. This cancellation puts an **End** to these **UCC contract Trust** by discharging the **CONTRACTORS** from all obligations as yet unperformed, because their **Contract Breaches, Deceptive Contract modifications, Defaults** and **Insurrections** against the **Owner** and **Principal**. **UCC cancellation** occurs when either party puts an **End** to the contract for a breach by the other. The effect is the same as that of **Termination**; EXCEPT that the **Canceling Party** also **Retains any remedy** for breach of the whole contract or any unperformed balance.

<u>The 3 Main Foreign UCC Contract Trust;</u> including all "GSA" SURETY Performance (SF-1418's) and Payment (SF-1416's) Bonds are to be liquidated per the Contract Modification SF-30 forms:
- "Certificate of Live Birth" registration # _____.
- Social Security Account per registration # _____.
- Military Selective Service Account per registration # _____.
- All other Sub UCC Contract Trust will be turned over to the Treasury UCC Contract Trust Agents upon their request.

      The **Contractors** and **Foreign Agents** are to be charged with **Income Tax Evasion** and **Violations against** the **14th Amendment "Federal Government - _American Commandment_"** by committing the **Commercial Acts of Insurrection** and **forced Servitude** against the **American "Federal Government" Principal Owner** and **Nation**.

      The **UCC Contract Trusts** are **Commanded** to be **Arrested** and **Processed** under this **Civil Arrest Warrant** and attached GSA Forms by the **National Treasury UCC Contract Trust Officers** and Liquidated along with all their Contractor Bonds and bound over for their final processing and deposit into the National Treasury Depositary per the IRS form 926, never to be resurrected into the **UCC Contract Trust** system again because of their Acts of Insurrection against the American People and this Nation. The **Reward** to this American Owner is to be in the form of a special National Treasury Credit Accessing account and an international nationally protected identification.

      As one of the **American "Federal Government"** - **We the People** of **Age** and an **Owner** of the American National Treasury by my right of birth inheritance; **I am** privately **attesting** to the **validity** of the above **Facts** and **Statements**, as **the Truth and nothing but the Truth** per the "National Government" Constitutional and Lawful "Federal Government" Amendment Laws for the United States of America.

Dated: _____

                                      Ordered, Posted and **Signed** by: _____
                                              American Federal Government UCC Contract Trust Owner – **Patrick; Devine**

1

Joe Sixpack, Claimant
c/o Temporary Mail Location:
c/o Laurie Rangel, Notary Public
c/o 607 Bootleg Rd.
Clarkdale, Arizona [86336]

First Mailing date

To the following Respondents:

Honorable Presiding Judge, or current office holder
in chambers
Judge, in chambers
Court
judge address
judge city, state
Certified Mail No.

Clerk of Court Clerk of Court
Court
address
city, state
Certified Mail No.

Re: Court name
Case No. No./Inmate No.

NOTICE TO AGENT IS NOTICE TO PRINCIPAL
NOTICE TO PRINCIPAL IS NOTICE TO AGENT

Dear Honorable Presiding Judge/Judge and other Respondents:

Please note, I have been informed the court sold bonds and/or securities bearing the name JOHN JAMES DOE, under SSN XXX-XX-XXXX, without my knowledge and consent, which I believe is securities fraud, as well as breach of your fiduciary duties. While I am not making such an accusation at this time, I am giving you an opportunity to rectify the situation. Enclosed you will find GSA forms OF90; Release of Lien on Real Property, OF91 Release of Personal Property from Escrow, SF28; Affidavit of Individual Surety, SF24 Bid Bond; SF25; Performance Bond and SF25A; Payment Bond. These bonds authorize you to order the release of the defendant/surety from prison and/or conditions of release. I demand to be released immediately. I also request that the record for Case Number(s) be amended to reflect the proper accounting to maintain the integrity of the data used in the national matching program.

It is my intent, through use of these government forms, to provide the remedy to settle and close the case and all associated accounts. It is my understanding that the defendant/trust has been an agency/vessel of the United States since August 12, 1949, and a resident of the State of Ohio. 26 USC 2031 (see 2652: definition of a trust - "any arrangement that has the effect of a trust is a trust whether it is called a trust or not') [Insinuation (Blks 8th and 5th), any time a deed is recorded by insinuation, it's called a donation](due to the fraud of the secrecy)[2046 Balance sheet], [1041 instruction booklet pg. 2,6 and 13] 6209 decoding manual; Title 12 sec 1813 L-1 "'Any note deposited in a demand deposit account becomes the equivalent of cash and is a cash proceed. RCW 62A.3-104(e)[UCC 3-104 E] "any note is a liability instrument or it can be treated as a draft" endorsed on the back as payee and Kentral-Que:Man was the payor as in a check I am the contracting officer for said trust, and no contracts are entered into without my signature. The trust known as JOHN JAMES DOE, account #XXX-XX-XXXX, has a bonded escrow account located at the DTC, from where all necessary funds may be accessed. (26 USC 2611 defines a "skip person" as a trust) including all incidents stemming from, relating to or having any relationship to from or with Lewis

County Washington for and on behalf of beneficiary Joe-Cold:Sixpack. This fraud was brought upon the Court when, as co-fiduciary trustees, they represented the plaintiff/ principal(s) to be the above listed plaintiff/principal(s) knowing that the Securities and Exchange Commission (SEC) SQ/SA and 424b5 prospectus filing(s) listed different entity(s) ownership(s) and I believe that no evidence to the contrary exists. The above named Administrators, Executors, Representatives and Fiduciary Trustee's while acting in their official capacities agree to hold the Grantor/Beneficiary Kentral-Que: Man harmless from any liability or loss by indemnification and bond from any and all possible taxable terminations, transfers, distributions, direct skips originating from the Legal Estate of the Decedent JOE COLD SIXPACK political commercial account No, 123456789. At the expiration of 72 HOURS of the date of this Indenture Agreement, Indemnity Bond, without the total and complete correction of the record will constitute a breach of contract with a summary judgment and an international commercial Notice of lien on the real and movable property, malpractice bond(s) and non performance bond(s) of each and every Co-Fiduciary/ Trustee and Co-Administrator, and all others similarly situated, et al, to be offered to the international community for execution.

This appointment will not be affected by the addition of additional Co-Administrators and Co-Fiduciary Trustees. from time to lime by the Grantor Beneficiary Kentral-Qee: Man, {Beatty v Guggenheim Exploration Co. 122 NE 378 (/9/9). 225 NY 380. 119 NE 575.223 NY 294 (/9/8). Land mark case all constructive trust} as they become known. FAILURE TO CORRECT THE RECORD AND SETTLE THE ACCOUNT WITHIN 72 HOURS will constitute a Trust ex maleficio and will result in a claim of Fiduciary Trust FRAUD for the wrongful conversion of beneficiary Stacy Paulette: McGuire's beneficial interest including the conversion of counterfeited securities and obstruction of justice with a claim to the Criminal Tax Division of the Internal Revenue Service for Criminal tax evasion of $500,000.00 including but not limited to many years in prison (Trezevant v. City of Tampa] and 1099OID and 1099C showing you as the recipient of the funds on this taxable instrument(s) and the international community for the execution of penalties for counterfeit securities issued against the Joe-Cold: Sixpack and without any AGREEMENT.

Pursuant to this Private Settlement Agreement Judgment:
IT IS DECLARED:
There now exists, a private contract between us and what I expect of you co-administrators and co-fiduciary trustees to remain on your side of the Declaration of Rights that precedes and attaches to the STATE OF WASHINGTON corporation constitution and that you remain in the state corporation constitution and out of my domain which is the declaration of the Bill of Rights and:

IT IS the intent herein that any conducted court proceedings are intended to be of competent jurisdiction and

IT IS the intent herein that Plaintiffs are corporations and

IT IS the intent herein that the Plaintiffs have failed to state a claim upon which relief can be granted [12(b)(6) and

IT IS the intent herein that the act of criminal barratry will be charged to the clerk of court and/or the court administrator for any reassignment of fiduciary duty by the court administrator and/or denial to the filing of this Private Settlement Agreement Order creating the denial of the right to access the court and

IT IS the intent herein that the act of criminal barratry will be charged to the judge/agent, clerk of court and/or court administrator for any controversy brought into this court in opposition to this Private Settlement Agreement and

---

Counterfeit Securities-- Pursuant to Title 18 USC § 4, of the commission of crimes cognizable by a court of the United States under Title 18 USC § 513 to wit: "513(a) Whoever makes.. utters or possesses a counterfeited security of a State or political subdivision thereof or of an organization with intent to deceive another person, organization, or government, shall be fined not more than $250,000.00 or imprisoned not more than ten years, or both.
See also Sections 23 11 , 23 14, and 2320 for additional fines and sanctions. Among the securities defined at 18 USC § 2311 is included "evidence of indebtedness" which, in a broad sense, may mean anything that is due and owing which would include a duty, obligation or right of action.

IT IS the intent herein that abuse of office, and official misconduct will occur for any failure of the clerk of court and/or court administrator and/or judge/agent to place this Private Settlement Agreement into the evidence file and

IT IS the intent herein that standard judicial operating procedures (SOP) can never over rule obstruction of justice or due process [Trezevant v. City of Tampa] and

IT IS the intent herein that any applicable damages shall be assessed at the rate previously set in Trezevant v. City of Tampa and

IT IS the intent herein that Administrators, Executors, Fiduciary Trustee's provide equal protection of the law as a Matter of Law and as a Matter of Record and

IT IS the intent herein that Administrators, Executors, Fiduciary Trustee's comply with Federal Congressional Legislation by not upholding recoupment and

IT IS the intent herein that the act of criminal barratry, abuse of office and/or official misconduct will be charged to the judge/agent, clerk of court and/or court administrator for any failure to acknowledge and deliver this Private Settlement Agreement judgment pursuant to the tenants herein and

IT IS the intent herein that this judgment is acknowledged by Plaintiffs and the Clerk of Court and

IT IS the intent herein that this judgment is entered with prejudice.
I have a right to redeem the bonds which the court and/or the prison sold in the Defendant/Inmate's name and social security number, therefore I am replacing those bonds with the enclosed bonds. I now own this case. The enclosed forms authorize you, and indeed, order you to:

1) RECALL all the bonds/securities which were previously sold in my name and social security number, and refund these monies to me, as those funds belong to me;
2) Obtain your funding through the bonds enclosed;
3) Send a statement of account showing a zero (0) balance, and a check for all bond monies previously received on this account, to the above mail location;
4) Release the defendant/surety from confinement and all conditions of supervised release, immediately.

THESE FORMS ARE NOT SUBJECT TO THE DISCRETION OF THE COURT or other recipients. If you think you have reason to reject these forms, you are required to **provide proof of claim via a sworn affidavit** as to why you are not required to accept the forms, or advise me of any defect you may find in the forms, and **provide your bond in support of your position.** Your failure to do so will be certified as fraud on your part, pursuant to *U.S. v. Tweel*. Please note that the court's comments are directed to Internal Revenue Service employees, and apply equally to all government employees.

> "Silence can only be equated with **fraud** when there is a legal or moral duty to speak, or when an inquiry left unanswered would be intentionally misleading. . . . We cannot condone this shocking conduct. . . . If this is the case we hope our message is clear. This sort of deception will not be tolerated and if this is routine it should be corrected immediately." *U.S. v. Tweel*, 550 F2d 297, 299-300

YOUR RESPONSIBILITY. I understand it may take 60 days to process the enclosed bonds, but I require a good-faith letter from you, **within 30 days of the postmark on this communication**, acknowledging receipt of the bonds and your good-faith intention to process the bonds and release me, or in the alternative, your affidavit and bond in support of your claim of a defect in the bonds. I am also requesting copies of the 1099-OIDs which were (or should have been) originally filed in regard to this case, as well as copies of IRS forms 706 and 709 which should have been filed. Your failure to respond within this time frame, in the manner stipulated, will comprise your default.

DEFAULT. Failure to respond pursuant to the said terms of response or specifically perform under the provisions of the enclosed government forms, i.e., credit and ledger claimant's tender of consideration, will comprise a default on your part. As an operation of law, a default will comprise your agreement, consent and confession to all of the terms, statements and facts herein and herewith, and all inclusions and indorsements, front and back, annexed hereto. Your default will comprise your confession **to holding all liability in the aforesaid matter, your stipulation that the above noted party has exhausted his/her administrative remedy, and your consent to all necessary collection procedures**. As well, your default will comprise your confession to securities fraud, tax fraud, breach of fiduciary duty and false imprisonment, and will be certified and reported to the Governor and the Comptroller of your State, the IRS and the United States Attorney in your area. Your default will comprise your agreement to the **arrest of your bond**, and to the filing of criminal complaints and/or a tort against you.

CONFESSION OF JUDGMENT: Default will comprise your agreement to accept and pay certain fees. **Your default is your agreement to pay a co-claimant fee of Fifty Million Dollars ($50,000,000.00) for the privilege of being joined as a co-Claimant against legal fiction JOHN JAMES DOE pursuant to each attempt to impair the Claim or stultify the Claimant (me) or Debtor (the Trust).**

Self-Executing Power of Attorney. To facilitate your strict compliance with all of the terms of the Contract, if you fail to correct the default within ten (10) days, you give, by remaining silent, unlimited power of attorney to Claimant to sign and execute for you regarding enforcement of your obligations under this Contract. In that event, you instruct and authorize the Claimant to **execute Respondent's signature(s) in representative capacity on a *Self-executing Power of Attorney* document.**

ESTOPPEL BY ACQUIESCENCE. Your Default will comprise your agreement that all issues pertaining to this Contact are deemed settled and closed **res judicata, stare decisis** and **collateral estoppel**, and as a result, **judgment by estoppel**, and therein you will be confessing to the criminal act of false imprisonment should you fail to release me.

WAIVER OF RIGHTS. CONFESSION OF JUDGMENT. Your Default will comprise your consent, agreement and confession to **waive any and all rights** to raise a controversy, appeal, object to, or controvert administratively or judicially any of the terms and provisions in this Contract or the estoppel, as well as your consent to serving as a successor surety for all obligations, commercial and corporeal, attributed to the account. Upon Default, you and your agents may not argue, controvert, or protest the finality of the administrative findings to which you have agreed unless such Waiver of Rights which follows is declined in writing. Any such argument or controversy will comprise your confession to Perjury, Enticement to Slavery and various crimes against humanity. The respondent's confession of judgment in the said amount is res judicata and stare decisis.
DENIAL OF WAIVER OF RIGHTS

I, _____, Respondent, hereby acknowledge that I have received, read and fully understand this administrative remedy presentment with attachments, endorsements and schedules, and do hereby reserve the right to raise a justiciable controversy by exhibiting verified proof of claim and loss no later than [must be within ten (10) days of date of signing below unless written permission for a longer period of time is obtained in writing from the Third Party Intervener/Real Party in Interest under injury]. In the event the said claim is honored, I further agree to settle all associated accounts to a zero ($-0-) Final Ending Balance.

        Respondent signature: _____, Date
_____

CERTIFICATION AND RECORDING OF NON-PERFORMANCE FOR EVIDENTIARY PURPOSES. For your protection, non-performance will be certified and recorded in the public record as evidence that **John James Doe has exhausted his/her administrative remedy and that you have elected to waive all rights to raise a controversy or claim immunity from collection proceedings, having declined the opportunity to plead.**

Thank you for your assistance with this matter.

        Sincerely,
        JOHN JAMES DOE
        Government-created ens legis/trust

        By: John James Doe
             Authorized Representative

RELEASE OF LIEN ON REAL PROPERTY

Whereas JOHN H. SMITH (STRAW MAN NAME), of   birth certificate number XXX XXXXXX   , by a bond
                    (Name)   (Place of Residence)
for the performance of U.S. Government Contract Number   SS# 123-45-6789   ,
became a surety for the complete and successful performance of said contract, which bond
includes a lien upon certain real property further described hereafter, and

Whereas said surety established the said lien upon the following property

PUT LEGAL DESCRIPTION OF PROPERTY HERE (FROM COUNTY PROPERTY TAX NOTICE)

and recorded this pledge on   COUNTY RECORDERS OFFICE
                                                          (Name of Land Records)
in the   STRAW MANS COUNTY   of   STRAW MANS STATE   ,
                    (Locality)   (State)
and

Whereas, I,   John Henry Smith (Real Mans Name)   , being a duly
authorized representative of the United States Government as a warranted contracting
officer, have determined that the lien is no longer required to ensure further performance of
the said Government contract or satisfaction of claims arising therefrom,
and

Whereas the surety remains liable to the United States Government for continued
performance of the said Government contract and satisfaction of claims pertaining thereto.

Now, therefore, this agreement witnesseth that the Government hereby releases the
aforementioned lien.

[Date]   (todays date)   [Signature] John Henry Smith, authorized representative
                                                          Seal   (right thumb print here)

AUTHORIZED FOR LOCAL REPRODUCTION

OPTIONAL FORM 90 (REV. 1-90) Prescribed
by GSA-FAR (48 CFR) 53.228(n)

RELEASE OF PERSONAL PROPERTY FROM ESCROW

Whereas PAUL BEN ZACCARDI   , of Birth certificate Ut.#218-1488 19562502397 by a bond
               (Name)   (Place of Residence)
for the performance of U.S. Government Contract Number   528-90-2509   ,
became a surety for the complete and successful performance of said contract, and Whereas said surety has placed certain personal property in escrow

in Account Number   CASE #041905712   on deposit

at   THIRD DISTRICT COURT , STATE OF UTAH SAL T LAKE COUNTY
                                 (Name of Financial Institution)

located at   450 SOUTH STATE STREET SALT LAKE CITY, UTAH 84111   , and
                               (Address of Financial Institution)

Whereas I,   Paul Ben   , being a duly authorized representative of the United States government as a warranted contracting officer, have determined that retention in escrow of the following property is no longer required to ensure further performance of the said Government contract or satisfaction of claims arising therefrom:

SEE CRIMINAL CASE #041905712 THIRD DISTRICT COURT 450 SO STATE STREET SLC UTAH 84111
SEE OPTIONAL FORM 90 RELEASE OF LIEN (ATTACHED)
SEE OPTIONAL FORM 91 RELEASE OF PERSONAL PROPERTY FROM ESCROW (ATTACHED)
SEE STANDARD FORM 24 BID BOND (ATTACHED)
SEE STANDARD FORM 25 PERFORMANCE BOND (ATTACHED)
SEE STANDARD FORM 25A PAYMENT BOND (ATTACHED)

and
Whereas the surety remains liable to the United States Government for the continued performance of the said Government contract and satisfaction of claims pertaining thereto.

Now, therefore, this agreement witnesseth that the Government hereby releases from escrow the property listed above, and directs the custodian of the aforementioned escrow account to deliver the listed property to the surety. If the listed property comprises the whole of the property placed in escrow in the aforementioned escrow account, the Government further directs the custodian to close the account and to return all property therein to the surety, along with any interest accruing which remains after the deduction of any fees lawfully owed to

. THIRD DISTRICT COURT , STATE OF UTAH SAL T LAKE COUNTY
          (Name of Financial Institution)

[Date]   [Signature]

                                     Seal

AUTHORIZED FOR LOCAL REPRODUCTION

OPTIONAL FORM 91 (1-90) Prescribed by
GSA-FAR (48 CFR) 53.228(o)

CONSENT OF SURETY	1. CONTRACT NUMBER	2. MODIFICATION NUMBER	3. DATED

The Surety (Co-Sureties) consents (consent) to the foregoing contract modification and agrees (agree) that its (their) bond or bonds shall apply and extend to the contract as modified or amended.

4. INDIVIDUAL PRINCIPAL	a. NAME OF PRINCIPAL			c. SIGNATURE	*(Affix Seal)*
	b. BUSINESS ADDRESS			d. TYPED NAME	
	STREET ADDRESS			e. TYPED TITLE	
	CITY	STATE	ZIP CODE	f. DATE THIS CONSENT EXECUTED	

5. CORPORATE PRINCIPAL	a. NAME OF PRINCIPAL			c. PERSON EXECUTING CONSENT *(Signature)*	*(Affix Seal)*
	b. BUSINESS ADDRESS			d. TYPED NAME	
	STREET ADDRESS			e. TYPED TITLE	
	CITY	STATE	ZIP CODE	f. DATE THIS CONSENT EXECUTED	

6. CORPORATE/INDIVIDUAL SURETY (CO-SURETIES)

The Principal or authorized representative shall execute this consent of surety with the modification to which it pertains. If the representative (e.g., attorney-in-fact) that signs the consent is not a member of the partnership, or joint venture, or an officer of the corporation involved, a Power-of-Attorney or a Certificate of Corporate Principal must accompany the consent.

	a. CORPORATE/INDIVIDUAL SURETY'S NAME			c. PERSON EXECUTING CONSENT *(Signature)*	*(Affix Seal)*
A	b. BUSINESS ADDRESS			d. TYPED NAME	
	STREET ADDRESS			e. TYPED TITLE	
	CITY	STATE	ZIP CODE	f. DATE THIS CONSENT EXECUTED	

	a. CORPORATE/INDIVIDUAL SURETY'S NAME			c. PERSON EXECUTING CONSENT *(Signature)*	*(Affix Seal)*
B	b. BUSINESS ADDRESS			d. TYPED NAME	
	STREET ADDRESS			e. TYPED TITLE	
	CITY	STATE	ZIP CODE	f. DATE THIS CONSENT EXECUTED	

	a. CORPORATE/INDIVIDUAL SURETY'S NAME			c. PERSON EXECUTING CONSENT *(Signature)*	*(Affix Seal)*
C	b. BUSINESS ADDRESS			d. TYPED NAME	
	STREET ADDRESS			e. TYPED TITLE	
	CITY	STATE	ZIP CODE	f. DATE THIS CONSENT EXECUTED	

(Add similar signature blocks on the back of this form if necessary for additional co-Sureties)

AUTHORIZED FOR LOCAL REPRODUCTION
Previous edition is usable

STANDARD FORM 1414 (REV. 5-97)
Prescribed by GSA - FAR (48 CFR) 53.228(k)

PAYMENT BOND FOR OTHER THAN CONSTRUCTION CONTRACTS
(See instructions on reverse)

DATE BOND EXECUTED *(Must not be later than bid opening date)*	OMB Control Number: 9000-0045 Expiration Date: 7/31/2016

Paperwork Reduction Act Statement - This information collection meets the requirements of 44 USC § 3507, as amended by section 2 of the Paperwork Reduction Act of 1995. You do not need to answer these questions unless we display a valid Office of Management and Budget (OMB) control number. The OMB control number for this collection is 9000-0045. We estimate that it will take 25 minutes to read the instructions, gather the facts, and answer the questions. Send only comments relating to our time estimate, including suggestions for reducing this burden, or any other aspects of this collection of information to: General Services Administration, Regulatory Secretariat Division (M1V1CB), 1800 F Street, NW, Washington, DC 20405.

PRINCIPAL *(Legal name and business address)*	TYPE OF ORGANIZATION *("X" one)*
	☐ INDIVIDUAL ☐ PARTNERSHIP
	☐ JOINT VENTURE ☐ CORPORATION
	STATE OF INCORPORATION

SURETY(IES) *(Name(s) and business address(es)) (Include ZIP code)*	PENAL SUM OF BOND			
	MILLION(S)	THOUSAND(S)	HUNDRED(S)	CENTS
	CONTRACT DATE		CONTRACT NUMBER	

We, the Principal and Surety(ies), are firmly bound to the United States of America (hereinafter called the Government) in the above penal sum. For payment of the penal sum, we bind ourselves, our heirs, executors, administrators, and successors, jointly and severally. However, where the Sureties are corporations acting as co-sureties, we, the Sureties, bind ourselves in such sum "jointly and severally" as well as "severally" only for the purpose of allowing a joint action or actions against any or all of us. For all other purposes, each Surety binds itself, jointly and severally with the Principal, for the payment of the sum shown opposite the name of the Surety. If no limit of liability is indicated, the limit of liability is the full amount of the penal sum.

CONDITIONS:

The Principal has entered into the contract identified above.

THEREFORE:

(a) The above obligation is void if the Principal promptly makes payment to all persons (claimants) having a contract relationship with the Principal or a subcontractor of the Principal for furnishing labor, material or both in the prosecution of the work provided for in the contract identified above and any duly authorized modifications thereof. Notice of those modifications to the Surety(ies) are waived.

(b) The above obligation shall remain in full force if the Principal does not promptly make payments to all persons (claimants) having a contract relationship with the principal or a subcontractor of the Principal for furnishing labor, material or both in the prosecution of the contract identified above. In these cases, persons not paid in full before the expiration of ninety (90) days after the date of which the last labor was performed or material furnishing, have a direct right of action against the principal and Surety(ies) on this bond for the sum or sums justly due. The claimant, however, may not bring a suit or any action -

(1) Unless claimant, other than one having a direct contract with the Principal, had given written notice to the Principal within ninety (90) days after the claimant did or performed the last of the work or labor, or furnished or supplied the last of the materials for which the claim is made. The notice is to state with substantial accuracy the amount claimed and the name of the party to whom the materials were furnished or supplied, or for whom the work or labor was done or performed. Such notice shall be served by mailing the same registered or certified mail, postage prepaid, in an envelope addressed to the Principal at any place where an office is regularly maintained for the transaction of business, or served in any manner in which legal process is served in the state in which the contract is being performed, save that such service need not be made by a public officer.

(2) After the expiration one (1) year following the date on which claimant did or performed the last of the work or labor, or furnished or supplied the last of the materials for which the suit is brought.

(3) Other than in the United States District court for the district in which the contract, or any part thereof, was performed and executed, and not elsewhere.

WITNESS:

The principal and Surety(ies) executed this bid bond and affixed their seals on the above date.

AUTHORIZED FOR LOCAL REPRODUCTION
Previous edition not usable

STANDARD FORM 1416 (REV. 10-98)
Prescribed by GSA-FAR (48 CFR) 53.228(m)

		PRINCIPAL			
SIGNATURE(S)	1. (Seal)	2. (Seal)	3. (Seal)		Corporate Seal
NAME(S) & TITLE(S) (Typed)	1.	2.	3.		

	INDIVIDUAL SURETY(IES)		
SIGNATURE(S)	1. (Seal)	2.	(Seal)
NAME(S) & TITLE(S) (Typed)	1.	2.	

		CORPORATE SURETY(IES)		
SURETY A	NAME & ADDRESS		STATE OF INCORPORATION	LIABILITY LIMIT $	Corporate Seal
	SIGNATURE(S)	1.	2.		
	NAME(S) & TITLE(S) (Typed)	1.	2.		
SURETY B	NAME & ADDRESS		STATE OF INCORPORATION	LIABILITY LIMIT $	Corporate Seal
	SIGNATURE(S)	1.	2.		
	NAME(S) & TITLE(S) (Typed)	1.	2.		

INSTRUCTIONS

1. This form is authorized for use when payment bonds are required under FAR (48 CFR) 28.103-3, i.e., payment bonds for other than construction contracts. Any deviation from this form will require the written approval of the Administrator of General Services.

2. Insert the full legal name and business address of the Principal in the space designated "Principal" on the face of the form. An authorized person shall sign the bond. Any person signing in a representative capacity (e.g., an attorney-in-fact) must furnish evidence of authority if that representative is not a member of the firm, partnership, or joint venture, or an officer of the corporation involved.

3. (a) Corporations executing the bond as sureties must appear on the Department of the Treasury's list of approved sureties and must act within the limitation listed therein. Where more than one corporate surety is involved, their names and addresses shall appear in the spaces (Surety A, Surety B, etc.) headed "CORPORATE SURETY(IES)." In the space designated "SURETY(IES)" on the face of the form, insert only the letter identification of the sureties.

   (b) Where individual Sureties are involved, a completed Affidavit of Individual Surety (Standard Form 28) for each individual surety, shall accompany the bond. The Government may require the surety to furnish additional substantiating information concerning its financial capability.

4. Corporations executing the bond shall affix their corporate seals. Individuals shall execute the bond opposite the word "Corporate Seal"; and shall affix an adhesive seal if executed in Maine, New Hampshire, or any other jurisdiction requiring adhesive seals.

5. Type the name and title of each person signing this bond in the space provided.

STANDARD FORM 1416 (REV. 10-98) **BACK**

PERFORMANCE BOND FOR OTHER THAN CONSTRUCTION CONTRACTS
(See instructions on reverse)

DATE BOND EXECUTED *(Must be same or later than date of contract)*	OMB Control Number: 9000-0045 Expiration Date: 7/31/2016

Paperwork Reduction Act Statement - This information collection meets the requirements of 44 USC § 3507, as amended by section 2 of the Paperwork Reduction Act of 1995. You do not need to answer these questions unless we display a valid Office of Management and Budget (OMB) control number. The OMB control number for this collection is 9000-0045. We estimate that it will take 25 minutes to read the instructions, gather the facts, and answer the questions. Send only comments relating to our time estimate, including suggestions for reducing this burden, or any other aspects of this collection of information to: General Services Administration, Regulatory Secretariat Division (M1V1CB), 1800 F Street, NW, Washington, DC 20405.

PRINCIPAL *(Legal name and business address)*	TYPE OF ORGANIZATION *("X" one)*
	☐ INDIVIDUAL ☐ PARTNERSHIP
	☐ JOINT VENTURE ☐ CORPORATION
	STATE OF INCORPORATION

SURETY(IES) *(Name(s) and business address(es))*	PENAL SUM OF BOND			
	MILLION(S)	THOUSAND(S)	HUNDRED(S)	CENTS
	CONTRACT DATE		CONTRACT NUMBER	
	OPTION DATE		OPTION NUMBER	

OBLIGATION:

We, the Principal and Surety(ies), are firmly bound to the United States of America (hereinafter called the Government) in the above penal sum. For payment of the penal sum, we bind ourselves, our heirs, executors, administrators, and successors, jointly and severally. However, where the Sureties are corporations acting as co-sureties, we, the Sureties, bind ourselves in such sum "jointly and severally" as well as "severally" only for the purpose of allowing a joint action or actions against any or all of us. For all other purposes, each Surety binds itself, jointly and severally with the Principal, for the payment of the sum shown opposite the name of the Surety. If no limit of liability is indicated, the limit of liability is the full amount of the penal sum.

CONDITIONS:

The principal has entered into the contract identified above.

THEREFORE:

The above obligation is void if the Principal: (1) Performs and fulfills all the undertakings, covenants, terms, conditions, and agreements of the contract during either the base term or an optional term of the contract and any extensions thereof that are granted by the Government, with or without notice to the Surety(ies), and during the life of any guaranty required under the contract, and (2) performs and fulfills all the undertakings, covenants, terms, conditions, and agreements of any and all duly authorized modifications of the contract that hereafter are made. Notice of those modifications to the Surety(ies) is waived.
The guaranty for a base term covers the initial period of performance of the contract and any extensions thereof excluding any options. The guaranty for an option term covers the period of performance for the option being exercised and any extensions thereof.
The failure of a surety to renew a bond for any option term shall not result in a default of any bond previously furnished covering any base or option term.

WITNESS:

The principal and Surety(ies) executed this performance bond and affixed their seals on the above date.

	PRINCIPAL		
SIGNATURE(S)	1. (Seal)	2. (Seal)	Corporate Seal
NAME(S) & TITLE(S) *(Typed)*	1.	2.	

	INDIVIDUAL SURETY(IES)	
SIGNATURE(S)	1. (Seal)	2. (Seal)
NAME(S) *(Typed)*	1.	2.

	CORPORATE SURETY(IES)		
SURETY A NAME & ADDRESS		STATE OF INCORPORATION	LIABILITY LIMIT $
SIGNATURE(S)	1.	2.	Corporate Seal
NAME(S) & TITLE(S) *(Typed)*	1.	2.	

AUTHORIZED FOR LOCAL REPRODUCTION
Previous edition not usable

STANDARD FORM 1418 (REV. 2-99)
Prescribed by GSA-FAR (48 CFR) 53.228(b)

SURETY B	NAME & ADDRESS		STATE OF INCORPORATION	LIABILITY LIMIT $	Corporate Seal
	SIGNATURE(S)	1.	2.		
	NAME(S) & TITLE(S) *(Typed)*	1.	2.		
SURETY C	NAME & ADDRESS		STATE OF INCORPORATION	LIABILITY LIMIT $	Corporate Seal
	SIGNATURE(S)	1.	2.		
	NAME(S) & TITLE(S) *(Typed)*	1.	2.		
SURETY D	NAME & ADDRESS		STATE OF INCORPORATION	LIABILITY LIMIT $	Corporate Seal
	SIGNATURE(S)	1.	2.		
	NAME(S) & TITLE(S) *(Typed)*	1.	2.		
SURETY E	NAME & ADDRESS		STATE OF INCORPORATION	LIABILITY LIMIT $	Corporate Seal
	SIGNATURE(S)	1.	2.		
	NAME(S) & TITLE(S) *(Typed)*	1.	2.		
SURETY F	NAME & ADDRESS		STATE OF INCORPORATION	LIABILITY LIMIT $	Corporate Seal
	SIGNATURE(S)	1.	2.		
	NAME(S) & TITLE(S) *(Typed)*	1.	2.		
SURETY G	NAME & ADDRESS		STATE OF INCORPORATION	LIABILITY LIMIT $	Corporate Seal
	SIGNATURE(S)	1.	2.		
	NAME(S) & TITLE(S) *(Typed)*	1.	2.		

BOND PREMIUM	RATE PER THOUSAND ($)	TOTAL ($)

INSTRUCTIONS

1. This form is authorized for use in connection with Government contracts. Any deviation from this form will require the written approval of the Administrator of General Services.

2. Insert the full legal name and business address of the Principal in the space designated "Principal" on the face of the form. An authorized person shall sign the bond. Any person signing in a representative capacity (e.g., an attorney-in-fact) must furnish evidence of authority if that representative is not a member of the firm, partnership, or joint venture, or an officer of the corporation involved.

3. (a) Corporations executing the bond as sureties must appear on the Department of the Treasury's list of approved sureties and must act within the limitation listed therein. Where more than one corporate surety is involved, their names and addresses shall appear in the spaces (Surety A, Surety B, etc.) headed "CORPORATE SURETY (IES)." In the space designated "SURETY(IES)" on the face of the form, insert only the letter identification of the sureties.

(b) Where individual sureties are involved, a completed Affidavit of Individual Surety (Standard Form 28) for each individual surety, shall accompany the bond. The Government may require the surety to furnish additional substantiating information concerning their financial capability.

4. Corporations executing the bond shall affix their corporate seals. Individuals shall execute the bond opposite the word "Corporate Seal", and shall affix an adhesive seal if executed in Maine, New Hampshire, or any other jurisdiction requiring adhesive seals.

5. Type the name and title of each person signing this bond in the space provided.

6. Unless otherwise specified, the bond shall be submitted to the contracting office that awarded the contract.

STANDARD FORM 1418 (REV. 2-99) **BACK**

BID BOND
(See instruction on reverse)

DATE BOND EXECUTED *(Must not be later than bid opening date)*

OMB NO.: **9000-0045**

Public reporting burden for this collection of information is estimated to average 25 minutes per response, including the time for reviewing instructions, searching existing data sources, gathering and maintaining the data needed, and completing and reviewing the collection of information. Send comments regarding this burden estimate or any other aspect of this collection of information, including suggestions for reducing this burden, to the FAR Secretariat (MVR), Federal Acquisition Policy Division, GSA, Washington, DC 20405.

PRINCIPAL *(Legal name and business address)*

TYPE OF ORGANIZATION *("X" one)*
☐ INDIVIDUAL   ☐ PARTNERSHIP
☐ JOINT VENTURE ☐ CORPORATION
STATE OF INCORPORATION

SURETY(IES) *(Name and business address)*

PENAL SUM OF BOND					BID IDENTIFICATION	
PERCENT OF BID PRICE	AMOUNT NOT TO EXCEED				BID DATE	INVITATION NO.
	MILLION(S)	THOUSAND(S)	HUNDRED(S)	CENTS		
					FOR *(Construction, Supplies, or Services)*	

OBLIGATION:

We, the Principal and Surety(ies) are firmly bound to the United States of America (hereinafter called the Government) in the above penal sum. For payment of the penal sum, we bind ourselves, our heirs, executors, administrators, and successors, jointly and severally. However, where the Sureties are corporations acting as co-sureties, we, the Sureties, bind ourselves in such sum "jointly and severally" as well as "severally" only for the purpose of allowing a joint action or actions against any or all of us. For all other purposes, each Surety binds itself, jointly and severally with the Principal, for the payment of the sum shown opposite the name of the Surety. If no limit of liability is indicated, the limit of liability is the full amount of the penal sum.

CONDITIONS:

The Principal has submitted the bid identified above.

THEREFORE:

The above obligation is void if the Principal - (a) upon acceptance by the Government of the bid identified above, within the period specified therein for acceptance (sixty (60) days if no period is specified), executes the further contractual documents and gives the bond(s) required by the terms of the bid as accepted within the time specified (ten (10) days if no period is specified) after receipt of the forms by the principal; or (b) in the event of failure to execute such further contractual documents and give such bonds, pays the Government for any cost of procuring the work which exceeds the amount of the bid.

Each Surety executing this instrument agrees that its obligation is not impaired by any extension(s) of the time for acceptance of the bid that the Principal may grant to the Government. Notice to the surety(ies) of extension(s) are waived. However, waiver of the notice applies only to extensions aggregating not more than sixty (60) calendar days in addition to the period originally allowed for acceptance of the bid.

WITNESS:

The Principal and Surety(ies) executed this bid bond and affixed their seals on the above date.

PRINCIPAL

SIGNATURE(S)	1.	2.	3.	Corporate Seal
	(Seal)	(Seal)	(Seal)	
NAME(S) & TITLE(S) (Typed)	1.	2.	3.	

INDIVIDUAL SURETY(IES)

SIGNATURE(S)	1.	2.	
		(Seal)	(Seal)
NAME(S) (Typed)	1.	2.	

CORPORATE SURETY(IES)

SURETY A	NAME & ADDRESS		STATE OF INC.	LIABILITY LIMIT ($)	
	SIGNATURE(S)	1.	2.		Corporate Seal
	NAME(S) & TITLE(S) (Typed)	1.	2.		

AUTHORIZED FOR LOCAL REPRODUCTION
Previous edition is usable

STANDARD FORM 24 (REV. 10-98)
Prescribed by GSA - FAR (48 CFR) 53.228(a)

		STATE OF INC.	LIABILITY LIMIT ($)	
SURETY B	NAME & ADDRESS			Corporate Seal
	SIGNATURE(S) 1.	2.		
	NAME(S) & TITLE(S) (Typed) 1.	2.		
SURETY C	NAME & ADDRESS	STATE OF INC.	LIABILITY LIMIT ($)	Corporate Seal
	SIGNATURE(S) 1.	2.		
	NAME(S) & TITLE(S) (Typed) 1.	2.		
SURETY D	NAME & ADDRESS	STATE OF INC.	LIABILITY LIMIT ($)	Corporate Seal
	SIGNATURE(S) 1.	2.		
	NAME(S) & TITLE(S) (Typed) 1.	2.		
SURETY E	NAME & ADDRESS	STATE OF INC.	LIABILITY LIMIT ($)	Corporate Seal
	SIGNATURE(S) 1.	2.		
	NAME(S) & TITLE(S) (Typed) 1.	2.		
SURETY F	NAME & ADDRESS	STATE OF INC.	LIABILITY LIMIT ($)	Corporate Seal
	SIGNATURE(S) 1.	2.		
	NAME(S) & TITLE(S) (Typed) 1.	2.		
SURETY G	NAME & ADDRESS	STATE OF INC.	LIABILITY LIMIT ($)	Corporate Seal
	SIGNATURE(S) 1.	2.		
	NAME(S) & TITLE(S) (Typed) 1.	2.		

INSTRUCTIONS

1. This form is authorized for use when a bid guaranty is required. Any deviation from this form will require the written approval of the Administrator of General Services.

2. Insert the full legal name and business address of the Principal in the space designated "Principal" on the face of the form. An authorized person shall sign the bond. Any person signing in a representative capacity (e.g., an attorney-in-fact) must furnish evidence of authority if that representative is not a member of the firm, partnership, or joint venture, or an officer of the corporation involved.

3. The bond may express penal sum as a percentage of the bid price. In these cases, the bond may state a maximum dollar limitation (e.g., (e.g., 20% of the bid price but the amount not to exceed _____ dollars).

4. (a) Corporations executing the bond as sureties must appear on the Department of the Treasury's list of approved sureties and must act within the limitation listed therein. where more than one corporate surety is involved, their names and addresses shall appear in the spaces (Surety A, Surety B, etc.) headed "CORPORATE SURETY(IES)." In the space designed "SURETY(IES)" on the face of the form, insert only the letter identification of the sureties.

(b) Where individual sureties are involved, a completed Affidavit of Individual surety (Standard Form 28), for each individual surety, shall accompany the bond. The Government may require the surety to furnish additional substantiating information concerning its financial capability.

5. Corporations executing the bond shall affix their corporate seals. Individuals shall execute the bond opposite the word "Corporate Seal"; and shall affix an adhesive seal if executed in Maine, New Hampshire, or any other jurisdiction requiring adhesive seals.

6. Type the name and title of each person signing this bond in the space provided.

7. In its application to negotiated contracts, the terms "bid" and "bidder" shall include "proposal" and "offeror."

PERFORMANCE BOND
(See instructions on reverse)

DATE BOND EXECUTED *(Must be same or later than date of contract)*	OMB No.: 9000-0045

Public reporting burden for this collection of information is estimated to average 25 minutes per response, including the time for reviewing instructions, searching existing data sources, gathering and maintaining the data needed, and completing and reviewing the collection of information. Send comments regarding this burden estimate or any other aspect of this collection of information, including suggestions for reducing this burden, to the FAR Secretariat (MVR), Federal Acquisition Policy Division, GSA, Washington, DC 20405

PRINCIPAL *(Legal name and business address)*	TYPE OF ORGANIZATION *("X" one)*
	☐ INDIVIDUAL ☐ PARTNERSHIP
	☐ JOINT VENTURE ☐ CORPORATION
	STATE OF INCORPORATION

SURETY(IES) *(Name(s) and business address(es))*	PENAL SUM OF BOND			
	MILLION(S)	THOUSAND(S)	HUNDRED(S)	CENTS
	CONTRACT DATE	CONTRACT NO.		

OBLIGATION:

We, the Principal and Surety(ies), are firmly bound to the United States of America (hereinafter called the Government) in the above penal sum. For payment of the penal sum, we bind ourselves, our heirs, executors, administrators, and successors, jointly and severally. However, where the Sureties are corporations acting as co-sureties, we, the Sureties, bind ourselves in such sum "jointly and severally" as well as "severally" only for the purpose of allowing a joint action or actions against any or all of us. For all other purposes, each Surety binds itself, jointly and severally with the Principal, for the payment of the sum shown opposite the name of the Surety. If no limit of liability is indicated, the limit of liability is the full amount of the penal sum.

CONDITIONS:

The Principal has entered into the contract identified above.

THEREFORE:

The above obligation is void if the Principal -

    (a)(1) Performs and fulfills all the undertakings, covenants, terms, conditions, and agreements of the contract during the original term of the contract and any extensions thereof that are granted by the Government, with or without notice to the Surety(ies), and during the life of any guaranty required under the contract, and (2) performs and fulfills all the undertakings, covenants, terms conditions, and agreements of any and all duly authorized modifications of the contract that hereafter are made. Notice of those modifications to the Surety(ies) are waived.

    (b) Pays to the Government the full amount of the taxes imposed by the Government, if the said contract is subject to the Miller Act, (40 U.S.C. 270a-270e), which are collected, deducted, or withheld from wages paid by the Principal in carrying out the construction contract with respect to which this bond is furnished.

WITNESS:

The Principal and Surety(ies) executed this performance bond and affixed their seals on the above date.

PRINCIPAL

SIGNATURE(S)	1. (Seal)	2. (Seal)	3. (Seal)	Corporate Seal
NAME(S) & TITLE(S) *(Typed)*	1.	2.	3.	

INDIVIDUAL SURETY(IES)

SIGNATURE(S)	1.	2. (Seal)	(Seal)
NAME(S) *(Typed)*	1.	2.	

CORPORATE SURETY(IES)

SURETY A	NAME & ADDRESS		STATE OF INC.	LIABILITY LIMIT $	
	SIGNATURE(S)	1.	2.		Corporate Seal
	NAME(S) & TITLE(S) *(Typed)*	1.	2.		

AUTHORIZED FOR LOCAL REPRODUCTION
Previous edition not usable

STANDARD FORM 25 (REV. 5-96)
Prescribed by GSA-FAR (48 CFR) 53.228(b)

CORPORATE SURETY(IES) (Continued)

			STATE OF INC.	LIABILITY LIMIT $	
SURETY B	NAME & ADDRESS				Corporate Seal
	SIGNATURE(S)	1.	2.		
	NAME(S) & TITLE(S) (Typed)	1.	2.		
SURETY C	NAME & ADDRESS		STATE OF INC.	LIABILITY LIMIT $	Corporate Seal
	SIGNATURE(S)	1.	2.		
	NAME(S) & TITLE(S) (Typed)	1.	2.		
SURETY D	NAME & ADDRESS		STATE OF INC.	LIABILITY LIMIT $	Corporate Seal
	SIGNATURE(S)	1.	2.		
	NAME(S) & TITLE(S) (Typed)	1.	2.		
SURETY E	NAME & ADDRESS		STATE OF INC.	LIABILITY LIMIT $	Corporate Seal
	SIGNATURE(S)	1.	2.		
	NAME(S) & TITLE(S) (Typed)	1.	2.		
SURETY F	NAME & ADDRESS		STATE OF INC.	LIABILITY LIMIT $	Corporate Seal
	SIGNATURE(S)	1.	2.		
	NAME(S) & TITLE(S) (Typed)	1.	2.		
SURETY G	NAME & ADDRESS		STATE OF INC.	LIABILITY LIMIT $	Corporate Seal
	SIGNATURE(S)	1.	2.		
	NAME(S) & TITLE(S) (Typed)	1.	2.		

BOND PREMIUM	RATE PER THOUSAND ($)	TOTAL ($)

INSTRUCTIONS

1. This form is authorized for use in connection with Government contracts. Any deviation from this form will require the written approval of the Administrator of General Services.

2. Insert the full legal name and business address of the Principal in the space designated "Principal" on the face of the form. An authorized person shall sign the bond. Any person signing in a representative capacity (e.g., an attorney-in-fact) must furnish evidence of authority if that representative is not a member of the firm, partnership, or joint venture, or an officer of the corporation involved.

3. (a) Corporations executing the bond as sureties must appear on the Department of the Treasury's list of approved sureties and must act within the limitation listed therein. Where more than one corporate surety is involved, their names and addresses shall appear in the spaces (Surety A, Surety B, etc.) headed "CORPORATE SURETY(IES)." In the space designated "SURETY(IES)" on the face of the form, insert only the letter identification of the sureties.

(b) Where individual sureties are involved, a completed Affidavit of Individual Surety (Standard Form 28) for each individual surety, shall accompany the bond. The Government may require the surety to furnish additional substantiating information concerning their financial capability.

4. Corporations executing the bond shall affix their corporate seals. Individuals shall execute the bond opposite the word "Corporate Seal", and shall affix an adhesive seal if executed in Maine, New Hampshire, or any other jurisdiction requiring adhesive seals.

5. Type the name and title of each person signing this bond in the space provided.

PAYMENT BOND
(See instructions on reverse)

DATE BOND EXECUTED *(Must be same or later than date of contract)*

OMB No.: 9000-0045

Public reporting burden for this collection of information is estimate to average 25 minutes per response, including the time for reviewing instructions, searching existing data sources, gathering and maintaining the data needed, and completing and reviewing the collection of information. Send comments regarding this burden estimate or any other aspect of this collection of information, including suggestions for reducing this burden, to the FAR Secretariat (MVR), Federal Acquisition Policy Division, GSA, Washington, DC 20405

PRINCIPAL *(Legal name and business address)*

TYPE OF ORGANIZATION *("X" one)*

☐ INDIVIDUAL ☐ PARTNERSHIP

☐ JOINT VENTURE ☐ CORPORATION

STATE OF INCORPORATION

SURETY(IES) *(Name(s) and business address(es))*

PENAL SUM OF BOND

MILLION(S)	THOUSAND(S)	HUNDRED(S)	CENTS

CONTRACT DATE	CONTRACT NO.

OBLIGATION:

We, the Principal and Surety(ies), are firmly bound to the United States of America (hereinafter called the Government) in the above penal sum. For payment of the penal sum, we bind ourselves, our heirs, executors, administrators, and successors, jointly and severally. However, where the Sureties are corporations acting as co-sureties, we, the Sureties, bind ourselves in such sum "jointly and severally" as well as "severally" only for the purpose of allowing a joint action or actions against any or all of us. For all other purposes, each Surety binds itself, jointly and severally with the Principal, for the payment of the sum shown opposite the name of the Surety. If no limit of liability is indicated, the limit of liability is the full amount of the penal sum.

CONDITIONS:

The above obligation is void if the Principal promptly makes payment to all persons having a direct relationship with the Principal or a subcontractor of the Principal for furnishing labor, material or both in the prosecution of the work provided for in the contract identified above, and any authorized modifications of the contract that subsequently are made. Notice of those modifications to the Surety(ies) are waived.

WITNESS:

The Principal and Surety(ies) executed this payment bond and affixed their seals on the above date.

PRINCIPAL

	1.	2.	3.	
SIGNATURE(S)	(Seal)	(Seal)	(Seal)	Corporate Seal
NAME(S) & TITLE(S) (Typed)	1.	2.	3.	

INDIVIDUAL SURETY(IES)

	1.	2.	
SIGNATURE(S)		(Seal)	(Seal)
NAME(S) (Typed)	1.	2.	

CORPORATE SURETY(IES)

			STATE OF INC.	LIABILITY LIMIT $	
SURETY A	NAME & ADDRESS				
	SIGNATURE(S)	1.	2.		Corporate Seal
	NAME(S) & TITLE(S) (Typed)	1.	2.		

AUTHORIZED FOR LOCAL REPRODUCTION
Previous edition is usable

STANDARD FORM 25A (REV. 10-98)
Prescribed by GSA-FAR (48 CFR) 53.2228(c)

CORPORATE SURETY(IES) *(Continued)*

			STATE OF INC.	LIABILITY LIMIT $	
SURETY B	NAME & ADDRESS				Corporate Seal
	SIGNATURE(S)	1.	2.		
	NAME(S) & TITLE(S) *(Typed)*	1.	2.		
SURETY C	NAME & ADDRESS		STATE OF INC.	LIABILITY LIMIT $	Corporate Seal
	SIGNATURE(S)	1.	2.		
	NAME(S) & TITLE(S) *(Typed)*	1.	2.		
SURETY D	NAME & ADDRESS		STATE OF INC.	LIABILITY LIMIT $	Corporate Seal
	SIGNATURE(S)	1.	2.		
	NAME(S) & TITLE(S) *(Typed)*	1.	2.		
SURETY E	NAME & ADDRESS		STATE OF INC.	LIABILITY LIMIT $	Corporate Seal
	SIGNATURE(S)	1.	2.		
	NAME(S) & TITLE(S) *(Typed)*	1.	2.		
SURETY F	NAME & ADDRESS		STATE OF INC.	LIABILITY LIMIT $	Corporate Seal
	SIGNATURE(S)	1.	2.		
	NAME(S) & TITLE(S) *(Typed)*	1.	2.		
SURETY G	NAME & ADDRESS		STATE OF INC.	LIABILITY LIMIT $	Corporate Seal
	SIGNATURE(S)	1.	2.		
	NAME(S) & TITLE(S) *(Typed)*	1.	2.		

INSTRUCTIONS

1. This form, for the protection of persons supplying labor and material, is used when a payment bond is required under the Act of August 24, 1935, 49 Stat. 793 (40 U.S.C. 270a-270e). Any deviation from this form will require the written approval of the Administrator of General Services.

2. Insert the full legal name and business address of the Principal in the space designated "Principal" on the face of the form. An authorized person shall sign the bond. Any person signing in a representative capacity (e.g., an attorney-in-fact) must furnish evidence of authority if that representative is not a member of the firm, partnership, or joint venture, or an officer of the corporation involved.

3. (a) Corporations executing the bond as sureties must appear on the Department of the Treasury's list of approved sureties and must act within the limitation listed therein. Where more than one corporate surety is involved, their names and addresses shall appear in the spaces (Surety A, Surety B, etc.) headed "CORPORATE SURETY(IES)." In the space designated "SURETY(IES)" on the face of the form, insert only the letter identification of the sureties.

(b) Where individual sureties are involved, a completed Affidavit of Individual Surety (Standard Form 28) for each individual surety, shall accompany the bond. The Government may require the surety to furnish additional substantiating information concerning their financial capability.

4. Corporations executing the bond shall affix their corporate seals. Individuals shall execute the bond opposite the word "Corporate Seal", and shall affix an adhesive seal if executed in Maine, New Hampshire, or any other jurisdiction requiring adhesive seals.

5. Type the name and title of each person signing this bond in the space provided.

STANDARD FORM 25A (REV.10-98) BACK

AFFIDAVIT OF INDIVIDUAL SURETY
(See instructions on reverse)

OMB No.: 9000-0001

Public reporting burden for this collection of information is estimated to average 3 hours per response, including the time for reviewing instructions, searching existing data sources, gathering and maintaining the data needed, and completing and reviewing the collection of information. Send comments regarding this burden estimate or any other aspect of this collection of information, including suggestions for reducing this burden, to the Regulatory Secretariat (MVA), Office of Acquisition Policy, GSA, Washington, DC 20405.

STATE OF UTAH

COUNTY OF Salt Lake County

SS.

I, the undersigned, being duly sworn, depose and say that I am: (1) the surety to the attached bond(s); (2) a citizen of the United States; and of full age and legally competent. I also depose and say that, concerning any stocks or bonds included in the assets listed below, that there are no restrictions on the resale of these securities pursuant to the registration provisions of Section 5 of the Securities Act of 1933. I recognize that statements contained herein concern a matter within the jurisdiction of an agency of the United States and the making of a false, fictitious or fraudulent statement may render the maker subject to prosecution under Title 18, United States Code Sections 1001 and 494. This affidavit is made to induce the United States of America to accept me as surety on the attached bond.

1. NAME *(First, Middle, Last) (Type or Print)* PAUL BEN ZACCARDI

2. HOME ADDRESS *(Number, Street, City, State, ZIP Code)*
2905 EAST DURBAN ROAD SANDY, UTAH 84093

3. TYPE AND DURATION OF OCCUPATION

4. NAME AND ADDRESS OF EMPLOYER *(If Self-employed, so State)*
THIRD DISTRICT COURT 450 SO. STATE STREET SLC, UTAH 84111

5. NAME AND ADDRESS OF INDIVIDUAL SURETY BROKER USED *(If any)*
(Number, Street, City, State, ZIP Code)

6. TELEPHONE NUMBER
HOME - 801-733-9777
BUSINESS -

7. THE FOLLOWING IS A TRUE REPRESENTATION OF THE ASSETS I HAVE PLEDGED TO THE UNITED STATES IN SUPPORT OF THE ATTACHED BOND:

(a) Real estate *(Include a legal description, street address and other identifying description; the market value; attach supporting certified documents Including recorded lien; evidence of title and the current tax assessment of the property. For market value approach, also provide a current appraisal.)*
SEE CRIMINAL CASE #041905712 THIRD DISTRICT COURT 450 SO STATE STREET SLC UTAH 84111
SEE OPTIONAL FORM 90 RELEASE OF LIEN (ATTACHED)
SEE OPTIONAL FORM 91 RELEASE OF PERSONAL PROPERTY FROM ESCROW (ATTACHED)
SEE STANDARD FORM 24 BID BOND (ATTACHED)
SEE STANDARD FORM 25 PERFORMANCE BOND (ATTACHED)
SEE STANDARD FORM 25A PAYMENT BOND (ATTACHED)

(b) Assets other than real estate *(describe the assets, the details of the escrow account, and attach certified evidence thereof).*
LETTER FROM SHAUNNA BRACKEN RESTTUTION AGENT UTAH STATE TAX COMMISION

8. IDENTIFY ALL MORTGAGES, LIENS, JUDGEMENTS, OR ANY OTHER ENCUMBRANCES INVOLVING SUBJECT ASSETS INCLUDING REAL ESTATE TAXES DUE AND PAYABLE.
SEE CRIMINAL CASE #041905712 THIRD DISTRICT COURT 450 SO STATE STREET SLC UTAH 84111
SEE OPTIONAL FORM 90 RELEASE OF LIEN (ATTACHED)
SEE OPTIONAL FORM 91 RELEASE OF PERSONAL PROPERTY FROM ESCROW (ATTACHED)
SEE STANDARD FORM 24 BID BOND (ATTACHED)
SEE STANDARD FORM 25 PERFORMANCE BOND (ATTACHED)
SEE STANDARD FORM 25A PAYMENT BOND (ATTACHED)

9. IDENTIFY ALL BONDS, INCLUDING BID GUARANTEES, FOR WHICH THE SUBJECT ASSETS HAVE BEEN PLEDGED WITHIN 3 YEARS PRIOR TO THE DATE OF EXECUTION OF THIS AFFIDAVIT.
SEE CRIMINAL CASE #041905712 THIRD DISTRICT COURT 450 SO STATE STREET SLC UTAH 84111
SEE OPTIONAL FORM 90 RELEASE OF LIEN (ATTACHED)
SEE OPTIONAL FORM 91 RELEASE OF PERSONAL PROPERTY FROM ESCROW (ATTACHED)
SEE STANDARD FORM 24 BID BOND (ATTACHED)
SEE STANDARD FORM 25 PERFORMANCE BOND (ATTACHED)
SEE STANDARD FORM 25A PAYMENT BOND (ATTACHED)

DOCUMENTATION OF THE PLEDGED ASSET MUST BE ATTACHED.

10. SIGNATURE

11. BOND AND CONTRACT TO WHICH THIS AFFIDAVIT RELATES
SEE OPTIONAL FORMS 90 AND 91 AND STANDARD FORMS 24, 25 AND 25A

12. SUBSCRIBED AND SWORN TO BEFORE ME AS FOLLOWS:

a. DATE OATH ADMINISTERED
MONTH   DAY   YEAR

b. CITY AND STATE *(Or other jurisdiction)*

Official Seal

c. NAME AND TITLE OF OFFICIAL ADMINISTERING OATH
(Type or print)

d. SIGNATURE (signature of notary public)

e. MY COMMISSION EXPIRES

AUTHORIZED FOR LOCAL REPRODUCTION Previous edition is not usable

STANDARD FORM 28 (REV. 6/2003)
Prescribed by GSA-FAR (48 CFR) 53.228(e)

INSTRUCTIONS

1. Individual sureties on bonds executed in connection with Government contracts must complete and submit this form with the bond. (See 48 CFR 28.203, 53.228(e).) The surety must have the completed form notarized.

2. No corporation, partnership, or other unincorporated association or firm, as such, is acceptable as an individual surety. Likewise, members of a partnership are not acceptable as sureties on bonds that a partnership or an association, or any co-partner or member thereof, is the principal obligor. However, stockholders of corporate principals are acceptable provided (a) their qualifications are independent of their stockholdings or financial interest therein, and (b) that the fact is expressed in the affidavit of justification. An individual surety will not include any financial interest in assets connected with the principal on the bond that this affidavit supports.

3. United States citizenship is a requirement for individual sureties for contracts and bonds when the contract is awarded in the United States. However, when the Contracting Officer is located in an outlying area or a foreign country, the individual surety is only required to be a permanent resident of the area or country in which the contracting officer is located.

4. All signatures of the affidavit submitted must be originals. Affidavits bearing reproduced signatures are not acceptable. An authorized person must sign the bond. Any person signing in a representative capacity (e.g., an attorney-in-fact) must furnish evidence of authority if that representative is not a member of a firm, partnership, or joint venture, or an officer of the corporation involved.

AMENDMENT OF SOLICITATION/MODIFICATION OF CONTRACT	1. CONTRACT ID CODE	PAGE OF PAGES
2. AMENDMENT/MODIFICATION NO.	3. EFFECTIVE DATE	4. REQUISITION/PURCHASE REQ. NO.	5. PROJECT NO. *(If applicable)*
6. ISSUED BY CODE		7. ADMINISTERED BY *(If other than Item 6)* CODE

8. NAME AND ADDRESS OF CONTRACTOR *(No., street, county, State and ZIP Code)*	(X)	9A. AMENDMENT OF SOLICITATION NO.
		9B. DATED *(SEE ITEM 11)*
		10A. MODIFICATION OF CONTRACT/ORDER NO.
		10B. DATED *(SEE ITEM 13)*
CODE FACILITY CODE		

11. THIS ITEM ONLY APPLIES TO AMENDMENTS OF SOLICITATIONS

☐ The above numbered solicitation is amended as set forth in Item 14. The hour and date specified for receipt of Offers ☐ is extended, ☐ is not extended.

Offers must acknowledge receipt of this amendment prior to the hour and date specified in the solicitation or as amended, by one of the following methods:
(a) By completing items 8 and 15, and returning _____ copies of the amendment; (b) By acknowledging receipt of this amendment on each copy of the offer submitted; or (c) By separate letter or telegram which includes a reference to the solicitation and amendment numbers. FAILURE OF YOUR ACKNOWLEDGMENT TO BE RECEIVED AT THE PLACE DESIGNATED FOR THE RECEIPT OF OFFERS PRIOR TO THE HOUR AND DATE SPECIFIED MAY RESULT IN REJECTION OF YOUR OFFER. If by virtue of this amendment your desire to change an offer already submitted, such change may be made by telegram or letter, provided each telegram or letter makes reference to the solicitation and this amendment, and is received prior to the opening hour and date specified.

12. ACCOUNTING AND APPROPRIATION DATA *(If required)*

13. THIS ITEM ONLY APPLIES TO MODIFICATION OF CONTRACTS/ORDERS.
IT MODIFIES THE CONTRACT/ORDER NO. AS DESCRIBED IN ITEM 14.

CHECK ONE	
☐	A. THIS CHANGE ORDER IS ISSUED PURSUANT TO: *(Specify authority)* THE CHANGES SET FORTH IN ITEM 14 ARE MADE IN THE CONTRACT ORDER NO. IN ITEM 10A.
☐	B. THE ABOVE NUMBERED CONTRACT/ORDER IS MODIFIED TO REFLECT THE ADMINISTRATIVE CHANGES *(such as changes in paying office, appropriation date, etc.)* SET FORTH IN ITEM 14, PURSUANT TO THE AUTHORITY OF FAR 43.103(b).
☐	C. THIS SUPPLEMENTAL AGREEMENT IS ENTERED INTO PURSUANT TO AUTHORITY OF:
☐	D. OTHER *(Specify type of modification and authority)*

E. IMPORTANT: Contractor ☐ is not, ☐ is required to sign this document and return _____ copies to the issuing office.

14. DESCRIPTION OF AMENDMENT/MODIFICATION *(Organized by UCF section headings, including solicitation/contract subject matter where feasible.)*

Except as provided herein, all terms and conditions of the document referenced in Item 9A or 10A, as heretofore changed, remains unchanged and in full force and effect.

15A. NAME AND TITLE OF SIGNER *(Type or print)*		16A. NAME AND TITLE OF CONTRACTING OFFICER *(Type or print)*	
15B. CONTRACTOR/OFFEROR	15C. DATE SIGNED	16B. UNITED STATES OF AMERICA	16C. DATE SIGNED
(Signature of person authorized to sign)		*(Signature of Contracting Officer)*	

NSN 7540-01-152-8070
Previous edition unusable

STANDARD FORM 30 (REV. 10-83)
Prescribed by GSA FAR (48 CFR) 53.243

INSTRUCTIONS

Instructions for items other than those that are self-explanatory, are as follows:

(a) Item 1 (Contract ID Code). Insert the contract type identification code that appears in the title block of the contract being modified.

(b) Item 3 (Effective date).

   (1) For a solicitation amendment, change order, or administrative change, the effective date shall be the issue date of the amendment, change order, or administrative change.

   (2) For a supplemental agreement, the effective date shall be the date agreed to by the contracting parties.

   (3) For a modification issued as an initial or confirming notice of termination for the convenience of the Government, the effective date and the modification number of the confirming notice shall be the same as the effective date and modification number of the initial notice.

   (4) For a modification converting a termination for default to a termination for the convenience of the Government, the effective date shall be the same as the effective date of the termination for default.

   (5) For a modification confirming the contacting officer's determination of the amount due in settlement of a contract termination, the effective date shall be the same as the effective date of the initial decision.

(c) Item 6 (Issued By). Insert the name and address of the issuing office. If applicable, insert the appropriate issuing office code in the code block.

(d) Item 8 (Name and Address of Contractor). For modifications to a contract or order, enter the contractor's name, address, and code as shown in the original contract or order, unless changed by this or a previous modification.

(e) Item 9, (Amendment of Solicitation No. - Dated), and 10, (Modification of Contract/Order No. - Dated). Check the appropriate box and in the corresponding blanks insert the number and date of the original solicitation, contract, or order.

(f) Item 12 (Accounting and Appropriation Data). When appropriate, indicate the impact of the modification on each affected accounting classification by inserting one of the following entries.

   (1) Accounting classification
       Net increase $ ....

   (2) Accounting classification
       Net decrease $ ....

   NOTE: If there are changes to multiple accounting classifications that cannot be placed in block 12, insert an asterisk and the words "See continuation sheet".

(g) Item 13. Check the appropriate box to indicate the type of modification. Insert in the corresponding blank the authority under which the modification is issued. Check whether or not contractor must sign this document. (See FAR 43.103.)

(h) Item 14 (Description of Amendment/Modification).

   (1) Organize amendments or modifications under the appropriate Uniform Contract Format (UCF) section headings from the applicable solicitation or contract. The UCF table of contents, however, shall not be set forth in this document

   (2) Indicate the impact of the modification on the overall total contract price by inserting one of the following entries:

      (i) Total contract price increased by $ ....

      (ii) Total contract price decreased by $ ....

      (iii) Total contract price unchanged.

   (3) State reason for modification.

   (4) When removing, reinstating, or adding funds, identify the contract items and accounting classifications.

   (5) When the SF 30 is used to reflect a determination by the contracting officer of the amount due in settlement of a contract terminated for the convenience of the Government, the entry in Item 14 of the modification may be limited to --

      (i) A reference to the letter determination; and

      (ii) A statement of the net amount determined to be due in settlement of the contract.

   (6) Include subject matter or short title of solicitation/contract where feasible.

(i) Item 16B. The contracting officer's signature is not required on solicitation amendments. The contracting officer's signature is normally affixed last on supplemental agreements.

STANDARD FORM 30 (REV. 10-83) **BACK**

Made in the USA
Monee, IL
04 May 2025

16865891R00046